W9-ABL-902

Bible Promises
to Treasure
for the New Millennium

Bible Promises
to Treasure
for the New Millennium

Inspiring

words

for every

occasion

BROADMAN
& HOLMAN
PUBLISHERS

Nashville, Tennessee

Bible Promises to Treasure for the New Millennium
©1999 Broadman & Holman Publishers,
Nashville, Tennessee
All rights reserved
Printed in Belgium

ISBN 0–8054–9389–1

Dewey Decimal Classification: 242.5
Subject Heading: CHRISTIAN LIFE QUOTATIONS

******

A note on the sources of quotations. When possible I have supplied
at least the book name from which contemporary quotes have
come. Yet even this is often impossible, since many came from my
"journal of jottings" over many years. Also, if a quote is from a
person who lived longer than fifty or so years ago, I've made no
attempt to cite the source. Such quotations are usually available in
any standard book of quotes.

******

Library of Congress Cataloging-in-Publication Data
Bible promises to treasure for the new millennium: inspiring words
   for every occasion / compiled by Gary Wilde.
      p. cm.
   Includes bibliographical references.
   ISBN 0–8054–9389–1
   1. Christian life—Quotations, maxims, etc.   I. Wilde, Gary
BV4513.B534   1999
242'.5 —dc21   99–28249
                                                                        CIP

1 2 3 4 5 6 03 02 01 00 99
S

Contents

Introduction

I remember as a child singing often at church: "Standing on the Promises of God." Or maybe it was mostly the adults who were singing; but I was standing next to them—my parents and all the others. I recall those faithful people joyfully reciting words they must surely have known by heart . . .

**When the howling storms
of doubt and fear assail,
By the living Word of God I shall prevail,
Standing on the promises of God.**

For years Downey Church, in sunny central Florida, had preached and taught the promises of God and believed in His goodness. From the *beginning—when the church building was a small tin-roofed, A-frame at the east end of a dirt road on the outskirts of Orlando—people would gather to stand on the immutable promises. Under the shiny tin roof, standing on the sandy-wooden floorboards, they melded their voices to the tunes of the upright piano and recalled God's goodness. Today, as the church there grows and thrives—now there is also a school and gymnasium—I can only attribute its vibrant life to a love of God's promises and the recognition that without the pledges that flow from the mouth of God, there is no church, no music, and no reason for either.*

The promises of God have always been the bedrock of Christian faith; for without God's sacred covenants with us, we cannot survive. In times of joy or heartache, in all our ups and downs, we keep coming back to that source of our life: the motivation for all our doing and the reason for our existence. It is the message of

God's mighty assurances: this life is not all there is, He will always be with us while we are here, and He will take us to be with Him someday. Yes, we do have priceless promises to keep close to our hearts!

My hope for you as you delve into this scriptural treasure chest is that you will grow deeper in love with the One who has spoken as no other ever could. With so many influences bombarding our minds each moment of the day, what could be better than to set aside a few moments of quiet to hear the still, small voice that constantly invites us into warm fellowship? We'll be richly rewarded if we truly listen to what that voice is saying. His words convey blessing and guidance, wisdom and warning, life for now and life everlasting. What incomparable grace!

Gary Wilde
Oviedo, Florida, 1999

One

Here's a New Day for Witness and Service

Entering a new Millennium is certainly a rare experience. Yet, on another level, that first day of 2000 is like any other day. No matter what momentous occasions may define our years— or our decades—on this earth, the simple truth remains: we can only live our lives one day at a time.

Today, Be Ready to Proclaim the Good News

Fight the temptation to be bashful about the Christian faith. Avoid a bashful brand of Christian that tiptoes up to people and hesitatingly suggests: "I may be wrong, but I'm afraid that if you do not repent after a fashion and receive Christ, so to speak, you might be damned, as it were."

—William A. Ward[1]

Declare his doings among the people, make mention that his name is exalted. . . .

Cry out and shout, thou inhabitant of Zion: for great is the Holy One of Israel in the midst of thee.

—Isaiah 12:4b, 6

For I will not dare to speak of any of those things which Christ hath not wrought by me, to make the Gentiles obedient, by word and deed,

Through mighty signs and wonders, by the power of the Spirit of God; so that from Jerusalem, and round about unto Illyricum, I have fully preached the gospel of Christ.

Yea, so have I strived to preach the gospel, not where Christ was named, lest I should build upon another man's foundation:

But as it is written, To whom he was not spoken of, they shall see: and they that have not heard shall understand.

—Romans 15:18–21

Stand therefore, having your loins girt about with truth, and having on the breastplate of righteousness;

And your feet shod with the preparation of the gospel of peace;

Above all, taking the shield of faith, wherewith ye shall be able to quench all the fiery darts of the wicked.

And take the helmet of salvation, and the sword of the Spirit, which is the word of God:

Praying always with all prayer and supplication in the Spirit, and watching thereunto with all perseverance and supplication for all saints;

And for me, that utterance may be given unto me, that I may open my mouth boldly, to make known the mystery of the gospel.

For which I am an ambassador in bonds: that therein I may speak boldly, as I ought to speak.

—Ephesians 6:14–20

Let us go forth therefore unto him without the camp, bearing his reproach.

For here have we no continuing city, but we seek one to come.

By him therefore let us offer the sacrifice of praise to God continually, that is, the fruit of our lips giving thanks to his name.

—Hebrews 13:13–15

That in every thing ye are enriched by him, in all utterance, and in all knowledge;

Even as the testimony of Christ was confirmed in you.

—1 Corinthians 1:5–6

Whosoever shall confess me before men, him shall the Son of man also confess before the angels of God:

But he that denieth me before men shall be denied before the angels of God.

—*Luke 12:8–9*

Keep Fighting Sin

Better to shun the bait
than struggle in the snare.

— *John Dryden*

The Lord shall deliver me from every evil work, and will preserve me unto his heavenly kingdom: to whom be glory for ever and ever.

—*2 Timothy 4:18*

For though we walk in the flesh, we do not war after the flesh:

(For the weapons of our warfare are not carnal, but mighty through God to the pulling down of strong holds;)

Casting down imaginations, and every high thing that exalteth itself against the knowledge of God, and bringing into captivity every thought to the obedience of Christ.

—2 Corinthians 10:3–5

Put on the whole armour of God, that ye may be able to stand against the wiles of the devil.

For we wrestle not against flesh and blood, but against principalities, against powers, against the rulers of the darkness of this world, against spiritual wickedness in high places.

Wherefore take unto you the whole armour of God, that ye may be able to withstand in the evil day, and having done all, to stand.

—Ephesians 6:11–13

Forasmuch then as the children are partakers of flesh and blood, he also himself likewise took part of the same; that through death he might destroy him that had the power of death, that is, the devil;

And deliver them who through fear of death were all their lifetime subject to bondage.

For verily he took not on him the nature of angels; but he took on him the seed of Abraham.

Wherefore in all things it behoved him to be made like unto his brethren, that he might be a merciful and faithful high priest in things pertaining to God, to make reconciliation for the sins of the people.

For in that he himself hath suffered being tempted, he is able to succour them that are tempted.

Wherefore, holy brethren, partakers of the heavenly calling, consider the Apostle and High Priest of our profession, Christ Jesus.

—*Hebrews 2:14–18; 3:1*

Look for People You Can Help

The value of compassion cannot be over-emphasized. Anyone can criticize. It takes a true believer to be compassionate. No greater burden can be borne by an individual than to know no one cares or understands.

—Arthur H. Stainback

And, behold, a certain lawyer stood up, and tempted him, saying, Master, what shall I do to inherit eternal life?

He said unto him, What is written in the law? how readest thou?

And he answering said, Thou shalt love the Lord thy God with all thy heart, and with all thy soul, and with all thy strength, and with all thy mind; and thy neighbour as thyself.

And he said unto him, Thou hast answered right: this do, and thou shalt live.

But he, willing to justify himself, said unto Jesus, And who is my neighbour?

And Jesus answering said, A certain man went down from Jerusalem to Jericho, and fell among thieves, which stripped him of his raiment, and wounded him, and departed, leaving him half dead.

And by chance there came down a certain priest that way: and when he saw him, he passed by on the other side.

And likewise a Levite, when he was at the place, came and looked on him, and passed by on the other side.

But a certain Samaritan, as he journeyed, came where he was: and when he saw him, he had compassion on him,

And went to him, and bound up his wounds, pouring in oil and wine, and set him on his own beast, and brought him to an inn, and took care of him.

And on the morrow when he departed, he took out two pence, and gave them to the host, and said unto him, Take care of him; and whatsoever thou spendest more, when I come again, I will repay thee.

Which now of these three, thinkest thou, was neighbour unto him that fell among the thieves?

And he said, He that shewed mercy on him. Then said Jesus unto him, Go, and do thou likewise.

—*Luke 10:25–37*

And when she had opened it, she saw the child: and, behold, the babe wept. And she had compassion on him, and said, This is one of the Hebrews' children.

Then said his sister to Pharaoh's daughter, Shall I go and call to thee a nurse of the Hebrew women, that she may nurse the child for thee?

And Pharaoh's daughter said to her, Go. And the maid went and called the child's mother.

And Pharaoh's daughter said unto her, Take this child away, and nurse it for me, and I will give thee thy wages. And the woman took the child, and nursed it.

And the child grew, and she brought him unto Pharaoh's daughter, and he became her son. And she called his name Moses: and she said, Because I drew him out of the water.

—*Exodus 2:6–10*

Wherefore, though I might be much bold in Christ to enjoin thee that which is convenient,

Yet for love's sake I rather beseech thee, being such an one as Paul the aged, and now also a prisoner of Jesus Christ.

I beseech thee for my son Onesimus, whom I have begotten in my bonds:

Which in time past was to thee unprofitable, but now profitable to thee and to me:

Whom I have sent again: thou therefore receive him, that is, mine own bowels:

Whom I would have retained with me, that in thy stead he might have ministered unto me in the bonds of the gospel:

But without thy mind would I do nothing; that thy benefit should not be as it were of necessity, but willingly.

For perhaps he therefore departed for a season, that thou shouldest receive him for ever;

Not now as a servant, but above a servant, a brother beloved, specially to me, but how much more unto thee, both in the flesh, and in the Lord?

If thou count me therefore a partner, receive him as myself.

If he hath wronged thee, or oweth thee ought, put that on mine account;

I Paul have written it with mine own hand, I will repay it: albeit I do not say to thee how thou owest unto me even thine own self besides.

Yea, brother, let me have joy of thee in the Lord: refresh my bowels in the Lord.

Having confidence in thy obedience I wrote unto thee, knowing that thou wilt also do more than I say.

—Philemon 8–21

And of some have compassion, making a difference:

And others save with fear, pulling them out of the fire; hating even the garment spotted by the flesh.

—Jude 1:22–23

And Serve in the Power of the Spirit

The word "Comforter" as applied to the Holy Spirit needs to be translated by some vigorous term. Literally, it means "with strength." Jesus promised His followers that "The Strengthener" would be with them forever. This promise is no lullaby for the faint-hearted. It is a blood transfusion for courageous living.

—E. Paul Hovey[2]

As every man hath received the gift, even so minister the same one to another, as good stewards of the manifold grace of God.

If any man speak, let him speak as the oracles of God; if any man minister, let him do it as of the ability which God giveth: that God in all things may be glorified through Jesus Christ, to whom be praise and dominion for ever and ever. Amen.

—1 Peter 4:10–11

Now there are diversities of gifts, but the same Spirit.

And there are differences of administrations, but the same Lord.

And there are diversities of operations, but it is the same God which worketh all in all.

But the manifestation of the Spirit is given to every man to profit withal.

For to one is given by the Spirit the word of wisdom; to another the word of knowledge by the same Spirit;

To another faith by the same Spirit; to another the gifts of healing by the same Spirit;

To another the working of miracles; to another prophecy; to another discerning of spirits; to another divers kinds of tongues; to another the interpretation of tongues:

But all these worketh that one and the selfsame Spirit, dividing to every man severally as he will.

For as the body is one, and hath many members, and all the members of that one body, being many, are one body: so also is Christ.

For by one Spirit are we all baptized into one body, whether we be Jews or Gentiles, whether we be bond or free; and have been all made to drink into one Spirit.

—1 Corinthians 12:4–13

For as we have many members in one body, and all members have not the same office:

So we, being many, are one body in Christ, and every one members one of another.

Having then gifts differing according to the grace that is given to us, whether prophecy, let us prophesy according to the proportion of faith;

Or ministry, let us wait on our ministering: or he that teacheth, on teaching;

Or he that exhorteth, on exhortation: he that giveth, let him do it with simplicity; he that ruleth, with diligence; he that sheweth mercy, with cheerfulness.

Let love be without dissimulation. Abhor that which is evil; cleave to that which is good.

Be kindly affectioned one to another with brotherly love; in honour preferring one another;

Not slothful in business; fervent in spirit; serving the Lord;

Rejoicing in hope; patient in tribulation; continuing instant in prayer;

Distributing to the necessity of saints; given to hospitality.

Bless them which persecute you: bless, and curse not.

Rejoice with them that do rejoice, and weep with them that weep.

Be of the same mind one toward another. Mind not high things, but condescend to men of low estate. Be not wise in your own conceits.

Recompense to no man evil for evil. Provide things honest in the sight of all men.

If it be possible, as much as lieth in you, live peaceably with all men.

—*Romans 12:4–18*

For the body is not one member, but many.

If the foot shall say, Because I am not the hand, I am not of the body; is it therefore not of the body?

And if the ear shall say, Because I am not the eye, I am not of the body; is it therefore not of the body?

If the whole body were an eye, where were the hearing? If the whole were hearing, where were the smelling?

But now hath God set the members every one of them in the body, as it hath pleased him.

And if they were all one member, where were the body?

But now are they many members, yet but one body.

And the eye cannot say unto the hand, I have no need of thee: nor again the head to the feet, I have no need of you.

Nay, much more those members of the body, which seem to be more feeble, are necessary:

And those members of the body, which we think to be less honourable, upon these we bestow more abundant honour; and our uncomely parts have more abundant comeliness.

For our comely parts have no need: but God hath tempered the body together, having given more abundant honour to that part which lacked:

That there should be no schism in the body; but that the members should have the same care one for another.

And whether one member suffer, all the members suffer with it; or one member be honoured, all the members rejoice with it.

—1 Corinthians 12:14–26

And he gave some, apostles; and some, prophets; and some, evangelists; and some, pastors and teachers;

For the perfecting of the saints, for the work of the ministry, for the edifying of the body of Christ.

—Ephesians 4:11–12

Two

*I*t's a *T*ime for *J*oy and *C*elebration!

*S*ome people speak of "Y2K" as purely an end-time event. It may very well be. After all, Jesus told us that no one can know for sure when the end will come. But are we to live in constant fear and anxiety? Of course not! Right until the end of the age—whether it be tomorrow or a hundred thousand years from now—our God is worthy of praise and joyful celebration.

Rejoice in This New Day!

Joy is one of the great Christian virtues. An uplifting part of the joy Jesus brought to His disciples was the joy of sharing. And sharing is of the essence of the Christian gospel. Let us enter into this joy . . . . The more we share, the richer is our own cooperation with God in His work.

—*Lucius C. Porter[1]*

This is the day which the LORD hath made; we will rejoice and be glad in it.

—*Psalm 118:24*

I will sing of the mercies of the LORD for ever: with my mouth will I make known thy faithfulness to all generations.

For I have said, Mercy shall be built up for ever: thy faithfulness shalt thou establish in the very heavens.

I have made a covenant with my chosen, I have sworn unto David my servant,

Thy seed will I establish for ever, and build up thy throne to all generations.

—Psalm 89:1–4

The LORD shall increase you more and more, you and your children.

Ye are blessed of the LORD which made heaven and earth.

The heaven, even the heavens, are the LORD's: but the earth hath he given to the children of men.

The dead praise not the LORD, neither any that go down into silence.

But we will bless the LORD from this time forth and for evermore. Praise the LORD.

—Psalm 115:14–18

In every thing give thanks: for this is the will of God in Christ Jesus concerning you.

—1 Thessalonians 5:18

Seek God's Will in This New Millennium

Whoso trusteth in the LORD, happy is he.

—Proverbs 16:20b

Stand every morning to thank and praise the LORD, and likewise at even.

—1 Chronicles 23:30

My soul shall be satisfied as with marrow and fatness; and my mouth shall praise thee with joyful lips.

—Psalm 63:5

Blessed is every one that feareth the LORD; that walketh in his ways.

For thou shalt eat the labour of thine hands: happy shalt thou be, and it shall be well with thee.

—Psalm 128:1–2

Acquaint now thyself with him, and be at peace: thereby good shall come unto thee.

Receive, I pray thee, the law from his mouth, and lay up his words in thine heart.

If thou return to the Almighty, thou shalt be built up, thou shalt put away iniquity far from thy tabernacles.

Then shalt thou lay up gold as dust, and the gold of Ophir as the stones of the brooks.

Yea, the Almighty shall be thy defence, and thou shalt have plenty of silver.

For then shalt thou have thy delight in the Almighty, and shalt lift up thy face unto God.

—Job 22:21–26

Happy art thou, O Israel: who is like unto thee, O people saved by the LORD, the shield of thy help, and who is the sword of thy excellency! and thine enemies shall be found liars unto thee; and thou shalt tread upon their high places.

—Deuteronomy 33:29

☽ *Make Time for Worship in the New Decade*

I will praise thee with my whole heart: before the gods will I sing praise unto thee.

I will worship toward thy holy temple, and praise thy name for thy lovingkindness and for thy truth: for thou hast magnified thy word above all thy name.

In the day when I cried thou answeredst me, and strengthenedst me with strength in my soul.

All the kings of the earth shall praise thee, O LORD, when they hear the words of thy mouth.

Yea, they shall sing in the ways of the LORD: for great is the glory of the LORD.

Though the LORD be high, yet hath he respect unto the lowly: but the proud he knoweth afar off.

Though I walk in the midst of trouble, thou wilt revive me: thou shalt stretch forth thine hand against the wrath of mine enemies, and thy right hand shall save me.

The LORD will perfect that which concerneth me: thy mercy, O LORD, endureth for ever: forsake not the works of thine own hands.

—*Psalm 138:1–8*

I will speak of the glorious honour of thy majesty, and of thy wondrous works.

And men shall speak of the might of thy terrible acts: and I will declare thy greatness.

They shall abundantly utter the memory of thy great goodness, and shall sing of thy righteousness.

The LORD is gracious, and full of compassion; slow to anger, and of great mercy.

The LORD is good to all: and his tender mercies are over all his works.

All thy works shall praise thee, O LORD; and thy saints shall bless thee.

They shall speak of the glory of thy kingdom, and talk of thy power;

To make known to the sons of men his mighty acts, and the glorious majesty of his kingdom.

Thy kingdom is an everlasting kingdom, and thy dominion endureth throughout all generations.

The LORD upholdeth all that fall, and raiseth up all those that be bowed down.

The eyes of all wait upon thee; and thou givest them their meat in due season.

Thou openest thine hand, and satisfiest the desire of every living thing.

The LORD is righteous in all his ways, and holy in all his works.

The LORD is nigh unto all them that call upon him, to all that call upon him in truth.

He will fulfil the desire of them that fear him: he also will hear their cry, and will save them.

The LORD preserveth all them that love him: but all the wicked will he destroy.

My mouth shall speak the praise of the LORD: and let all flesh bless his holy name for ever and ever.

—*Psalm 145:5–21*

Recall God's Past Goodness

O Lord, who lends me life, lend me a heart replete with thankfulness.

—*William Shakespeare*

I will extol thee, O LORD; for thou hast lifted me up, and hast not made my foes to rejoice over me.

O LORD my God, I cried unto thee, and thou hast healed me.

O LORD, thou hast brought up my soul from the grave: thou hast kept me alive, that I should not go down to the pit.

Sing unto the LORD, O ye saints of his, and give thanks at the remembrance of his holiness.

For his anger endureth but a moment; in his favour is life: weeping may endure for a night, but joy cometh in the morning.

And in my prosperity I said, I shall never be moved.

—Psalm 30:1–6

Good and upright is the LORD: therefore will he teach sinners in the way.

The meek will he guide in judgment: and the meek will he teach his way.

All the paths of the LORD are mercy and truth unto such as keep his covenant and his testimonies.

—Psalm 25:8–10

O LORD our Lord, how excellent is thy name in all the earth! who hast set thy glory above the heavens.

Out of the mouth of babes and sucklings hast thou ordained strength because of thine enemies, that thou mightest still the enemy and the avenger.

When I consider thy heavens, the work of thy fingers, the moon and the stars, which thou hast ordained;

What is man, that thou art mindful of him? and the son of man, that thou visitest him?

For thou hast made him a little lower than the angels, and hast crowned him with glory and honour.

Thou madest him to have dominion over the works of thy hands; thou hast put all things under his feet:

All sheep and oxen, yea, and the beasts of the field;

The fowl of the air, and the fish of the sea, and whatsoever passeth through the paths of the seas.

O LORD our Lord, how excellent is thy name in all the earth!

—*Psalm 8:1–9*

How precious also are thy thoughts unto me, O God! how great is the sum of them!

If I should count them, they are more in number than the sand: when I awake, I am still with thee.

—Psalm 139:17–18

Afterward shall the children of Israel return, and seek the LORD their God, and David their king; and shall fear the LORD and his goodness in the latter days.

—Hosea 3:5

Or what man is there of you, whom if his son ask bread, will he give him a stone?

Or if he ask a fish, will he give him a serpent?

If ye then, being evil, know how to give good gifts unto your children, how much more shall your Father which is in heaven give good things to them that ask him?

—Matthew 7:9–11

☉ *He Provides Great Blessings on Earth*

By terrible things in righteousness wilt thou answer us, O God of our salvation;

who art the confidence of all the ends of the earth, and of them that are afar off upon the sea:

Which by his strength setteth fast the mountains; being girded with power:

Which stilleth the noise of the seas, the noise of their waves, and the tumult of the people.

They also that dwell in the uttermost parts are afraid at thy tokens: thou makest the outgoings of the morning and evening to rejoice.

Thou visitest the earth, and waterest it: thou greatly enrichest it with the river of God, which is full of water: thou preparest them corn, when thou hast so provided for it.

Thou waterest the ridges thereof abundantly: thou settlest the furrows thereof: thou makest it soft with showers: thou blessest the springing thereof.

Thou crownest the year with thy goodness; and thy paths drop fatness.

They drop upon the pastures of the wilderness: and the little hills rejoice on every side.

The pastures are clothed with flocks; the valleys also are covered over with corn; they shout for joy, they also sing.

—*Psalm 65:5–13*

Then shall he give the rain of thy seed, that thou shalt sow the ground withal; and bread of the increase of the earth, and it shall be fat and plenteous: in that day shall thy cattle feed in large pastures.

The oxen likewise and the young asses that ear the ground shall eat clean provender, which hath been winnowed with the shovel and with the fan.

And there shall be upon every high mountain, and upon every high hill, rivers and streams of waters in the day of the great slaughter, when the towers fall.

Moreover the light of the moon shall be as the light of the sun, and the light of the sun shall be sevenfold, as the light of seven days, in the day that the LORD bindeth up the breach of his people, and healeth the stroke of their wound.

—*Isaiah 30:23–26*

Bring ye all the tithes into the storehouse, that there may be meat in mine house, and prove me now herewith, saith the Lord of hosts, if I will not open you the windows of heaven, and pour you out a blessing, that there shall not be room enough to receive it.

And I will rebuke the devourer for your sakes, and he shall not destroy the fruits of your ground; neither shall your vine cast her fruit before the time in the field, saith the Lord of hosts.

And all nations shall call you blessed: for ye shall be a delightsome land, saith the Lord of hosts.

—*Malachi 3:10–12*

And he said unto his disciples, Therefore I say unto you, Take no thought for your life, what ye shall eat; neither for the body, what ye shall put on.

The life is more than meat, and the body is more than raiment.

Consider the ravens: for they neither sow nor reap; which neither have storehouse nor barn; and God feedeth them: how much more are ye better than the fowls?

And which of you with taking thought can add to his stature one cubit?

If ye then be not able to do that thing which is least, why take ye thought for the rest?

Consider the lilies how they grow: they toil not, they spin not; and yet I say unto you, that Solomon in all his glory was not arrayed like one of these.

If then God so clothe the grass, which is to day in the field, and to morrow is cast into the oven; how much more will he clothe you, O ye of little faith?

And seek not ye what ye shall eat, or what ye shall drink, neither be ye of doubtful mind.

For all these things do the nations of the world seek after: and your Father knoweth that ye have need of these things.

But rather seek ye the kingdom of God; and all these things shall be added unto you.

—*Luke 12:22–31*

⏰ *He Gives Us All Spiritual Blessings*

Every good gift and every perfect gift is
from above, and cometh down from the
Father of lights, with whom is no
variableness, neither shadow of turning.

Of his own will begat he us with the word
of truth, that we should be a kind of
firstfruits of his creatures.

—*James 1:17–18*

Blessed be the God and Father of our
Lord Jesus Christ, who hath blessed us with
all spiritual blessings in heavenly places in
Christ:

According as he hath chosen us in him
before the foundation of the world, that we
should be holy and without blame before
him in love:

Having predestinated us unto the
adoption of children by Jesus Christ to
himself, according to the good pleasure of
his will,

To the praise of the glory of his grace, wherein he hath made us accepted in the beloved.

In whom we have redemption through his blood, the forgiveness of sins, according to the riches of his grace;

Wherein he hath abounded toward us in all wisdom and prudence;

Having made known unto us the mystery of his will, according to his good pleasure which he hath purposed in himself:

That in the dispensation of the fulness of times he might gather together in one all things in Christ, both which are in heaven, and which are on earth; even in him:

In whom also we have obtained an inheritance, being predestinated according to the purpose of him who worketh all things after the counsel of his own will:

That we should be to the praise of his glory, who first trusted in Christ.

In whom ye also trusted, after that ye heard the word of truth, the gospel of your salvation: in whom also after that ye believed, ye were sealed with that holy Spirit of promise,

Which is the earnest of our inheritance until the redemption of the purchased possession, unto the praise of his glory.

—*Ephesians 1:3–14*

Thy shoes shall be iron and brass; and as thy days, so shall thy strength be.

There is none like unto the God of Jeshurun, who rideth upon the heaven in thy help, and in his excellency on the sky.

The eternal God is thy refuge, and underneath are the everlasting arms.

—*Deuteronomy 33:25–27a*

The righteous shall flourish like the palm tree: he shall grow like a cedar in Lebanon.

Those that be planted in the house of the LORD shall flourish in the courts of our God.

They shall still bring forth fruit in old age; they shall be fat and flourishing.

—*Psalm 92:12–14*

Strengthened with all might, according to his glorious power, unto all patience and longsuffering with joyfulness;

Giving thanks unto the Father, which hath made us meet to be partakers of the inheritance of the saints in light.

—*Colossians 1:11–12*

For they verily for a few days chastened us after their own pleasure; but he for our profit, that we might be partakers of his holiness.

Now no chastening for the present seemeth to be joyous, but grievous: nevertheless afterward it yieldeth the peaceable fruit of righteousness unto them which are exercised thereby.

—*Hebrews 12:10–11*

Shout for Joy!

The day is lost on which one has not laughed.

—*French proverb*

Sing, O ye heavens; for the LORD hath done it: shout, ye lower parts of the earth:

break forth into singing, ye mountains, O forest, and every tree therein: for the LORD hath redeemed Jacob, and glorified himself in Israel.

—Isaiah 44:23

O clap your hands, all ye people; shout unto God with the voice of triumph.

For the LORD most high is terrible; he is a great King over all the earth.

He shall subdue the people under us, and the nations under our feet.

He shall choose our inheritance for us, the excellency of Jacob whom he loved. Selah.

God is gone up with a shout, the LORD with the sound of a trumpet.

Sing praises to God, sing praises: sing praises unto our King, sing praises.

For God is the King of all the earth: sing ye praises with understanding.

God reigneth over the heathen: God sitteth upon the throne of his holiness.

The princes of the people are gathered together, even the people of the God of

Abraham: for the shields of the earth belong unto God: he is greatly exalted.

—*Psalm 47:1–9*

Cry out and shout, thou inhabitant of Zion: for great is the Holy One of Israel in the midst of thee.

—*Isaiah 12:6*

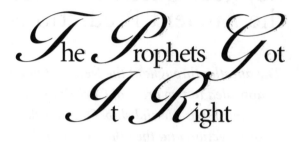

Three

The Prophets Got It Right

The credibility of a prophet's vision of the faraway future is always determined by the accuracy of his predictions about the near future. And the standard is quite high: nothing less than one hundred percent will do. Here are some of the prophecies in the Old Testament that have already been fulfilled in the New.

Rejoice! Christ Fulfilled the Ancient Predictions

The apostles throughout the New Testament appealed to two areas of Christ's life to establish His Messiahship. One was the Resurrection and the other was fulfilled messianic prophecy. The Old Testament, written over a 1,500 year period, contains several hundred references to the coming Messiah. All of these were fulfilled in Christ and they establish a solid confirmation of His credentials as the Messiah.

—*Josh McDowell*[1]

Beginning at Moses and all the prophets, he expounded unto them in all the scriptures the things concerning himself.

—*Luke 24:27*

⏲ *About His First Advent*

The sceptre shall not depart from Judah, nor a lawgiver from between his feet, until

Shiloh come; and unto him shall the
gathering of the people be.

—*Genesis 49:10*

And the Redeemer shall come to Zion,
and unto them that turn from transgression
in Jacob, saith the LORD.

—*Isaiah 59:20*

I shall see him, but not now: I shall
behold him, but not nigh: there shall come
a Star out of Jacob, and a Sceptre shall rise
out of Israel, and shall smite the corners of
Moab, and destroy all the children of Sheth.

—*Numbers 24:17*

Behold, I will send my messenger, and he
shall prepare the way before me: and the
Lord, whom ye seek, shall suddenly come to
his temple, even the messenger of the
covenant, whom ye delight in: behold, he
shall come, saith the LORD of hosts.

—*Malachi 3:1*

Why do the heathen rage, and the people
imagine a vain thing?

The kings of the earth set themselves, and the rulers take counsel together, against the LORD, and against his anointed, saying,

Let us break their bands asunder, and cast away their cords from us.

He that sitteth in the heavens shall laugh: the Lord shall have them in derision.

Then shall he speak unto them in his wrath, and vex them in his sore displeasure.

Yet have I set my king upon my holy hill of Zion.

I will declare the decree: the LORD hath said unto me, Thou art my Son; this day have I begotten thee.

—*Psalm 2:1–7*

Therefore thus saith the Lord GOD, Behold, I lay in Zion for a foundation a stone, a tried stone, a precious corner stone, a sure foundation: he that believeth shall not make haste.

—*Isaiah 28:16*

⊙ *About His Birth and Early Years*

Therefore the Lord himself shall give you a sign; Behold, a virgin shall conceive, and bear a son, and shall call his name Immanuel.

Butter and honey shall he eat, that he may know to refuse the evil, and choose the good.

—Isaiah 7:14–15

But thou, Bethlehem Ephratah, though thou be little among the thousands of Judah, yet out of thee shall he come forth unto me that is to be ruler in Israel; whose goings forth have been from of old, from everlasting.

—Micah 5:2

For unto us a child is born, unto us a son is given: and the government shall be upon his shoulder: and his name shall be called Wonderful, Counsellor, The mighty God, The everlasting Father, The Prince of Peace.

—Isaiah 9:6

The kings of Tarshish and of the isles shall bring presents: the kings of Sheba and Seba shall offer gifts.

Yea, all kings shall fall down before him: all nations shall serve him.

For he shall deliver the needy when he crieth; the poor also, and him that hath no helper.

He shall spare the poor and needy, and shall save the souls of the needy.

He shall redeem their soul from deceit and violence: and precious shall their blood be in his sight.

And he shall live, and to him shall be given of the gold of Sheba: prayer also shall be made for him continually; and daily shall he be praised.

—Psalm 72:10–15

And the Gentiles shall come to thy light, and kings to the brightness of thy rising.

Lift up thine eyes round about, and see: all they gather themselves together, they come to thee: thy sons shall come from far, and thy daughters shall be nursed at thy side.

Then thou shalt see, and flow together, and thine heart shall fear, and be enlarged; because the abundance of the sea shall be converted unto thee, the forces of the Gentiles shall come unto thee.

The multitude of camels shall cover thee, the dromedaries of Midian and Ephah; all they from Sheba shall come: they shall bring gold and incense; and they shall shew forth the praises of the LORD.

—Isaiah 60:3–6

☐ *About His Mission and Office*

And I will bless them that bless thee, and curse him that curseth thee: and in thee shall all families of the earth be blessed.

—Genesis 12:3

The LORD thy God will raise up unto thee a Prophet from the midst of thee, of thy brethren, like unto me; unto him ye shall hearken;

According to all that thou desiredst of the LORD thy God in Horeb in the day of the assembly, saying, Let me not hear again the voice of the LORD my God, neither let me see this great fire any more, that I die not.

And the LORD said unto me, They have well spoken that which they have spoken.

I will raise them up a Prophet from among their brethren, like unto thee, and will put my words in his mouth; and he shall speak unto them all that I shall command him.

—Deuteronomy 18:15–18

And in that day there shall be a root of Jesse, which shall stand for an ensign of the people; to it shall the Gentiles seek: and his rest shall be glorious.

—Isaiah 11:10

Out of Jacob shall come he that shall have dominion, and shall destroy him that remaineth of the city.

—Numbers 24:19

Behold my servant, whom I uphold; mine elect, in whom my soul delighteth; I have put my spirit upon him: he shall bring forth judgment to the Gentiles.

—Isaiah 42:1

And the spirit of the LORD shall rest upon him, the spirit of wisdom and understanding, the spirit of counsel and might, the spirit of knowledge and of the fear of the LORD.

—Isaiah 11:2

The Spirit of the Lord GOD is upon me; because the LORD hath anointed me to preach good tidings unto the meek; he hath sent me to bind up the brokenhearted, to proclaim liberty to the captives, and the opening of the prison to them that are bound;

To proclaim the acceptable year of the LORD, and the day of vengeance of our God; to comfort all that mourn.

—Isaiah 61:1–2

Say to them that are of a fearful heart, Be strong, fear not: behold, your God will come with vengeance, even God with a recompence; he will come and save you.

Then the eyes of the blind shall be opened, and the ears of the deaf shall be unstopped.

Then shall the lame man leap as an hart, and the tongue of the dumb sing: for in the wilderness shall waters break out, and streams in the desert.

—*Isaiah 35:4–6*

And many nations shall come, and say, Come, and let us go up to the mountain of the LORD, and to the house of the God of Jacob; and he will teach us of his ways, and we will walk in his paths: for the law shall go forth of Zion, and the word of the LORD from Jerusalem.

—*Micah 4:2*

For he is our peace, who hath made both one, and hath broken down the middle wall of partition between us;

Having abolished in his flesh the enmity, even the law of commandments contained in ordinances; for to make in himself of twain one new man, so making peace;

And that he might reconcile both unto God in one body by the cross, having slain the enmity thereby:

And came and preached peace to you which were afar off, and to them that were nigh.

—Ephesians 2:14–17

For the zeal of thine house hath eaten me up; and the reproaches of them that reproached thee are fallen upon me.

—Psalm 69:9

⏱ *About His Suffering and Death*

My God, my God, why hast thou forsaken me? why art thou so far from helping me, and from the words of my roaring? . . .

I am poured out like water, and all my bones are out of joint: my heart is like wax; it is melted in the midst of my bowels.

My strength is dried up like a potsherd; and my tongue cleaveth to my jaws; and thou hast brought me into the dust of death.

For dogs have compassed me: the assembly of the wicked have inclosed me: they pierced my hands and my feet.

I may tell all my bones: they look and stare upon me.

They part my garments among them, and cast lots upon my vesture.

But be not thou far from me, O LORD: O my strength, haste thee to help me.

—*Psalm 22:1, 14–19*

But in mine adversity they rejoiced, and gathered themselves together: yea, the abjects gathered themselves together against me, and I knew it not; they did tear me, and ceased not:

With hypocritical mockers in feasts, they gnashed upon me with their teeth.

Lord, how long wilt thou look on? rescue my soul from their destructions, my darling from the lions.

I will give thee thanks in the great congregation: I will praise thee among much people.

Let not them that are mine enemies wrongfully rejoice over me: neither let them wink with the eye that hate me without a cause.

For they speak not peace: but they devise deceitful matters against them that are quiet in the land.

Yea, they opened their mouth wide against me, and said, Aha, aha, our eye hath seen it.

—*Psalm 35:15–21*

Deliver me not over unto the will of mine enemies: for false witnesses are risen up against me, and such as breathe out cruelty.

—*Psalm 27:12*

False witnesses did rise up; they laid to my charge things that I knew not.

—*Psalm 35:11*

For the mouth of the wicked and the mouth of the deceitful are opened against me: they have spoken against me with a lying tongue.

—Psalm 109:2

I gave my back to the smiters, and my cheeks to them that plucked off the hair: I hid not my face from shame and spitting.

—Isaiah 50:6

They gave me also gall for my meat; and in my thirst they gave me vinegar to drink.

—Psalm 69:21

I became also a reproach unto them: when they looked upon me they shaked their heads.

—Psalm 109:25

They weighed for my price thirty pieces of silver.

—Zechariah 11:12b

He keepeth all his bones: not one of them is broken.

—Psalm 34:20

Surely he hath borne our griefs, and carried our sorrows: yet we did esteem him stricken, smitten of God, and afflicted.

But he was wounded for our transgressions, he was bruised for our iniquities: the chastisement of our peace was upon him; and with his stripes we are healed.

All we like sheep have gone astray; we have turned every one to his own way; and the Lord hath laid on him the iniquity of us all.

He was oppressed, and he was afflicted, yet he opened not his mouth: he is brought as a lamb to the slaughter, and as a sheep before her shearers is dumb, so he openeth not his mouth.

He was taken from prison and from judgment: and who shall declare his generation? for he was cut off out of the land of the living: for the transgression of my people was he stricken.

And he made his grave with the wicked, and with the rich in his death; because he had done no violence, neither was any deceit in his mouth.

Yet it pleased the LORD to bruise him; he hath put him to grief: when thou shalt make his soul an offering for sin, he shall see his seed, he shall prolong his days, and the pleasure of the LORD shall prosper in his hand.

He shall see of the travail of his soul, and shall be satisfied: by his knowledge shall my righteous servant justify many; for he shall bear their iniquities.

Therefore will I divide him a portion with the great, and he shall divide the spoil with the strong; because he hath poured out his soul unto death: and he was numbered with the transgressors; and he bare the sin of many, and made intercession for the transgressors.

—*Isaiah 53:4–12*

Sacrifice and offering thou didst not desire; mine ears hast thou opened: burnt offering and sin offering hast thou not required.

Then said I, Lo, I come: in the volume of the book it is written of me,

I delight to do thy will, O my God: yea,
thy law is within my heart.

—Psalm 40:6–8

⏱ *About His Resurrection*

I have set the LORD always before me:
because he is at my right hand, I shall not
be moved.

Therefore my heart is glad, and my glory
rejoiceth: my flesh also shall rest in hope.

For thou wilt not leave my soul in hell;
neither wilt thou suffer thine Holy One to
see corruption.

—Psalm 16:8–10

O LORD, thou hast brought up my soul
from the grave: thou hast kept me alive, that
I should not go down to the pit.

—Psalm 30:3

But thou, O LORD, be merciful unto me,
and raise me up, that I may requite them.

—Psalm 41:10

I shall not die, but live, and declare the works of the LORD.

—*Psalm 118:17*

① *About His Ascension*

Thou hast ascended on high, thou hast led captivity captive: thou hast received gifts for men; yea, for the rebellious also, that the LORD God might dwell among them.

—*Psalm 68:18*

The LORD said unto my Lord, Sit thou at my right hand, until I make thine enemies thy footstool.

—*Psalm 110:1*

Thou wilt shew me the path of life: in thy presence is fulness of joy; at thy right hand there are pleasures for evermore.

—*Psalm 16:11*

Lift up your heads, O ye gates; and be ye lift up, ye everlasting doors; and the King of glory shall come in.

—*Psalm 24:7*

Open to me the gates of righteousness: I will go into them, and I will praise the LORD:

—Psalm 118:19

① *About His Second Advent and Everlasting Dominion*

And it shall come to pass, when thy days be expired that thou must go to be with thy fathers, that I will raise up thy seed after thee, which shall be of thy sons; and I will establish his kingdom.

He shall build me an house, and I will stablish his throne for ever.

I will be his father, and he shall be my son: and I will not take my mercy away from him, as I took it from him that was before thee:

But I will settle him in mine house and in my kingdom for ever: and his throne shall be established for evermore.

—1 Chronicles 17:11–14

And in the days of these kings shall the God of heaven set up a kingdom, which shall never be destroyed: and the kingdom shall not be left to other people, but it shall break in pieces and consume all these kingdoms, and it shall stand for ever.

—*Daniel 2:44*

I saw in the night visions, and, behold, one like the Son of man came with the clouds of heaven, and came to the Ancient of days, and they brought him near before him.

And there was given him dominion, and glory, and a kingdom, that all people, nations, and languages, should serve him: his dominion is an everlasting dominion, which shall not pass away, and his kingdom that which shall not be destroyed.

—*Daniel 7:13–14*

For he hath put all things under his feet. But when he saith all things are put under him, it is manifest that he is excepted, which did put all things under him.

And when all things shall be subdued
unto him, then shall the Son also himself be
subject unto him that put all things under
him, that God may be all in all.

—1 Corinthians 15:27–28

Thy throne, O God, is for ever and ever:
the sceptre of thy kingdom is a right sceptre.

Thou lovest righteousness, and hatest
wickedness: therefore God, thy God, hath
anointed thee with the oil of gladness above
thy fellows.

—Psalm 45:6–7

For I know their works and their
thoughts: it shall come, that I will gather all
nations and tongues; and they shall come,
and see my glory.

—Isaiah 66:18

But in the last days it shall come to pass,
that the mountain of the house of the Lord
shall be established in the top of the
mountains, and it shall be exalted above the
hills; and people shall flow unto it.

—Micah 4:1

And I will pour upon the house of David, and upon the inhabitants of Jerusalem, the spirit of grace and of supplications: and they shall look upon me whom they have pierced, and they shall mourn for him, as one mourneth for his only son, and shall be in bitterness for him, as one that is in bitterness for his firstborn.

—Zechariah 12:10

He shall have dominion also from sea to sea, and from the river unto the ends of the earth.

—Psalm 72:8

Of the increase of his government and peace there shall be no end, upon the throne of David, and upon his kingdom, to order it, and to establish it with judgment and with justice from henceforth even for ever. The zeal of the LORD of hosts will perform this.

—Isaiah 9:7

Four

Jesus Made Predictions, Too!

Many are talking about what has happened in the past and what might happen in the future. But have you listened closely to Jesus on these matters? Here's your chance to hear, once again, the wisest and greatest Prophet of all.

He Talked About What Would Happen

What is before us, we know not, whether we shall live or die; but this we know, that all things are ordered and sure. Everything is

*ordered with unerring wisdom and
unbounded love, by Thee, our God, who art
love. Grant us in all things to see thy hand;
through Jesus Christ our Lord.*

—*Charles Simeon*[1]

⏱ *His Rejection and Death*

And as Moses lifted up the serpent in the
wilderness, even so must the Son of man be
lifted up:

That whosoever believeth in him should
not perish, but have eternal life.

—*John 3:14–15*

And he said unto them, Ye will surely say
unto me this proverb, Physician, heal
thyself: whatsoever we have heard done in
Capernaum, do also here in thy country.

And he said, Verily I say unto you, No
prophet is accepted in his own country.

But I tell you of a truth, many widows
were in Israel in the days of Elias, when the
heaven was shut up three years and six
months, when great famine was throughout
all the land;

But unto none of them was Elias sent, save unto Sarepta, a city of Sidon, unto a woman that was a widow.

And many lepers were in Israel in the time of Eliseus the prophet; and none of them was cleansed, saving Naaman the Syrian.

—*Luke 4:23–27*

And he answered and told them, Elias verily cometh first, and restoreth all things; and how it is written of the Son of man, that he must suffer many things, and be set at nought.

But I say unto you, That Elias is indeed come, and they have done unto him whatsoever they listed, as it is written of him.

—*Mark 9:12–13*

And while they abode in Galilee, Jesus said unto them, The Son of man shall be betrayed into the hands of men:

And they shall kill him, and the third day he shall be raised again. And they were exceeding sorry.

—*Matthew 17:22–23*

Then Jesus six days before the passover came to Bethany, where Lazarus was which had been dead, whom he raised from the dead.

There they made him a supper; and Martha served: but Lazarus was one of them that sat at the table with him.

Then took Mary a pound of ointment of spikenard, very costly, and anointed the feet of Jesus, and wiped his feet with her hair: and the house was filled with the odour of the ointment.

Then saith one of his disciples, Judas Iscariot, Simon's son, which should betray him,

Why was not this ointment sold for three hundred pence, and given to the poor?

This he said, not that he cared for the poor; but because he was a thief, and had the bag, and bare what was put therein.

Then said Jesus, Let her alone: against the day of my burying hath she kept this.

For the poor always ye have with you; but me ye have not always.

—John 12:1–8

Then he took unto him the twelve, and said unto them, Behold, we go up to Jerusalem, and all things that are written by the prophets concerning the Son of man shall be accomplished.

For he shall be delivered unto the Gentiles, and shall be mocked, and spitefully entreated, and spitted on:

And they shall scourge him, and put him to death: and the third day he shall rise again.

—Luke 18:31–33

Ye know that after two days is the feast of the passover, and the Son of man is betrayed to be crucified.

—Matthew 26:2

And as they did eat, he said, Verily I say unto you, that one of you shall betray me.

And they were exceeding sorrowful, and began every one of them to say unto him, Lord, is it I?

And he answered and said, He that dippeth his hand with me in the dish, the same shall betray me.

The Son of man goeth as it is written of him: but woe unto that man by whom the Son of man is betrayed! it had been good for that man if he had not been born.

—*Matthew 26:21–24*

I speak not of you all: I know whom I have chosen: but that the scripture may be fulfilled, He that eateth bread with me hath lifted up his heel against me.

Now I tell you before it come, that, when it is come to pass, ye may believe that I am he.

—*John 13:18–19*

And he cometh the third time, and saith unto them, Sleep on now, and take your rest: it is enough, the hour is come; behold, the Son of man is betrayed into the hands of sinners.

Rise up, let us go; lo, he that betrayeth me is at hand.

—*Mark 14:41–42*

Then said Jesus unto Peter, Put up thy sword into the sheath: the cup which my Father hath given me, shall I not drink it?

⏲ *His Resurrection*

After this he went down to Capernaum, he, and his mother, and his brethren, and his disciples: and they continued there not many days.

And the Jews' passover was at hand, and Jesus went up to Jerusalem,

And found in the temple those that sold oxen and sheep and doves, and the changers of money sitting:

And when he had made a scourge of small cords, he drove them all out of the temple, and the sheep, and the oxen; and poured out the changers' money, and overthrew the tables;

And said unto them that sold doves, Take these things hence; make not my Father's house an house of merchandise.

And his disciples remembered that it was written, The zeal of thine house hath eaten me up.

Then answered the Jews and said unto him, What sign shewest thou unto us, seeing that thou doest these things?

Jesus answered and said unto them, Destroy this temple, and in three days I will raise it up.

—*John 2:12–19*

And after six days Jesus taketh Peter, James, and John his brother, and bringeth them up into an high mountain apart,

And was transfigured before them: and his face did shine as the sun, and his raiment was white as the light.

And, behold, there appeared unto them Moses and Elias talking with him.

Then answered Peter, and said unto Jesus, Lord, it is good for us to be here: if thou wilt, let us make here three tabernacles; one for thee, and one for Moses, and one for Elias.

While he yet spake, behold, a bright cloud overshadowed them: and behold a voice out of the cloud, which said, This is my beloved Son, in whom I am well pleased; hear ye him.

And when the disciples heard it, they fell on their face, and were sore afraid.

And Jesus came and touched them, and said, Arise, and be not afraid.

And when they had lifted up their eyes, they saw no man, save Jesus only.

And as they came down from the mountain, Jesus charged them, saying, Tell the vision to no man, until the Son of man be risen again from the dead.

—*Matthew 17:1–9*

And as they were eating, Jesus took bread, and blessed it, and brake it, and gave it to the disciples, and said, Take, eat; this is my body.

And he took the cup, and gave thanks, and gave it to them, saying, Drink ye all of it;

For this is my blood of the new testament, which is shed for many for the remission of sins.

But I say unto you, I will not drink henceforth of this fruit of the vine, until that day when I drink it new with you in my Father's kingdom.

And when they had sung an hymn, they went out into the mount of Olives.

Then saith Jesus unto them, All ye shall be offended because of me this night: for it is written, I will smite the shepherd, and the sheep of the flock shall be scattered abroad.

But after I am risen again, I will go before you into Galilee.

—*Matthew 26:26–32*

☉ *His Ascension and Glory*

And he said unto them, Can ye make the children of the bridechamber fast, while the bridegroom is with them?

But the days will come, when the bridegroom shall be taken away from them, and then shall they fast in those days.

—*Luke 5:34–35*

Then said Jesus unto them, Yet a little while am I with you, and then I go unto him that sent me.

Ye shall seek me, and shall not find me: and where I am, thither ye cannot come.

—*John 7:33–34*

Then said Jesus again unto them, I go my way, and ye shall seek me, and shall die in your sins: whither I go, ye cannot come.

—*John 8:21*

Therefore, when he was gone out, Jesus said, Now is the Son of man glorified, and God is glorified in him.

If God be glorified in him, God shall also glorify him in himself, and shall straightway glorify him.

Little children, yet a little while I am with you. Ye shall seek me: and as I said unto the Jews, Whither I go, ye cannot come; so now I say to you.

—*John 13:31–33*

Ye have heard how I said unto you, I go away, and come again unto you. If ye loved me, ye would rejoice, because I said, I go unto the Father: for my Father is greater than I.

And now I have told you before it come to pass, that, when it is come to pass, ye might believe.

—*John 14:28–29*

But now I go my way to him that sent me; and none of you asketh me, Whither goest thou?

But because I have said these things unto you, sorrow hath filled your heart.

—*John 16:5–6*

Now Jesus knew that they were desirous to ask him, and said unto them, Do ye enquire among yourselves of that I said, A little while, and ye shall not see me: and again, a little while, and ye shall see me?

Verily, verily, I say unto you, That ye shall weep and lament, but the world shall rejoice: and ye shall be sorrowful, but your sorrow shall be turned into joy.

A woman when she is in travail hath sorrow, because her hour is come: but as soon as she is delivered of the child, she remembereth no more the anguish, for joy that a man is born into the world.

And ye now therefore have sorrow: but I will see you again, and your heart shall rejoice, and your joy no man taketh from you.

And in that day ye shall ask me nothing. Verily, verily, I say unto you, Whatsoever ye shall ask the Father in my name, he will give it you.

Hitherto have ye asked nothing in my name: ask, and ye shall receive, that your joy may be full.

These things have I spoken unto you in proverbs: but the time cometh, when I shall no more speak unto you in proverbs, but I shall shew you plainly of the Father.

At that day ye shall ask in my name: and I say not unto you, that I will pray the Father for you:

For the Father himself loveth you, because ye have loved me, and have believed that I came out from God.

I came forth from the Father, and am come into the world: again, I leave the world, and go to the Father.

—*John 16:19–28*

Jesus saith unto her, Touch me not; for I am not yet ascended to my Father: but go to my brethren, and say unto them, I ascend unto my Father, and your Father; and to my God, and your God.

—John 20:17

☉ *His Resurrected People*

Verily, verily, I say unto you, The hour is coming, and now is, when the dead shall hear the voice of the Son of God: and they that hear shall live.

For as the Father hath life in himself; so hath he given to the Son to have life in himself;

And hath given him authority to execute judgment also, because he is the Son of man.

Marvel not at this: for the hour is coming, in the which all that are in the graves shall hear his voice,

And shall come forth; they that have done good, unto the resurrection of life; and they that have done evil, unto the resurrection of damnation.

—John 5:25–29

And Jesus answering said unto them, The children of this world marry, and are given in marriage:

But they which shall be accounted worthy to obtain that world, and the resurrection from the dead, neither marry, nor are given in marriage:

Neither can they die any more: for they are equal unto the angels; and are the children of God, being the children of the resurrection.

Now that the dead are raised, even Moses shewed at the bush, when he calleth the Lord the God of Abraham, and the God of Isaac, and the God of Jacob.

For he is not a God of the dead, but of the living: for all live unto him.

—*Luke 20:34–38*

◷ *His Coming in Glory*

Jesus saw Nathanael coming to him, and saith of him, Behold an Israelite indeed, in whom is no guile!

Nathanael saith unto him, Whence knowest thou me? Jesus answered and said unto him, Before that Philip called thee, when thou wast under the fig tree, I saw thee.

Nathanael answered and saith unto him, Rabbi, thou art the Son of God; thou art the King of Israel.

Jesus answered and said unto him, Because I said unto thee, I saw thee under the fig tree, believest thou? thou shalt see greater things than these.

And he saith unto him, Verily, verily, I say unto you, Hereafter ye shall see heaven open, and the angels of God ascending and descending upon the Son of man.

—John 1:47–51

For the Son of man shall come in the glory of his Father with his angels; and then he shall reward every man according to his works.

Verily I say unto you, There be some standing here, which shall not taste of death, till they see the Son of man coming in his kingdom.

—Matthew 16:27–28

Let not your heart be troubled: ye believe in God, believe also in me.

In my Father's house are many mansions: if it were not so, I would have told you. I go to prepare a place for you.

And if I go and prepare a place for you, I will come again, and receive you unto myself; that where I am, there ye may be also.

And whither I go ye know, and the way ye know.

—John 14:1–4

And he said unto them, With desire I have desired to eat this passover with you before I suffer:

For I say unto you, I will not any more eat thereof, until it be fulfilled in the kingdom of God.

And he took the cup, and gave thanks, and said, Take this, and divide it among yourselves:

For I say unto you, I will not drink of the fruit of the vine, until the kingdom of God shall come.

—Luke 22:15–18

He Made Promises to His Followers

*O Lord Jesus Christ, who didst invite the
heavy laden to come to thee, and didst
promise to give them rest and never to cast
them out, help us so to come to thee that we
find rest in thee, and so to believe thy
promise that we may know that thou hast
received us, for the glory of thy name, who
with the Father and the Holy Spirit art ever
worthy to be trusted and adored.*

—*John R.W. Stott*[2]

⏲ *You'll Have Authority!*

And Jesus answered and said unto him,
Blessed art thou, Simon Bar-jona: for flesh
and blood hath not revealed it unto thee,
but my Father which is in heaven.

And I say also unto thee, That thou art
Peter, and upon this rock I will build my
church; and the gates of hell shall not
prevail against it.

And I will give unto thee the keys of the kingdom of heaven: and whatsoever thou shalt bind on earth shall be bound in heaven: and whatsoever thou shalt loose on earth shall be loosed in heaven.

—*Matthew 16:17–19*

And he said unto them, I beheld Satan as lightning fall from heaven.

Behold, I give unto you power to tread on serpents and scorpions, and over all the power of the enemy: and nothing shall by any means hurt you.

Notwithstanding in this rejoice not, that the spirits are subject unto you; but rather rejoice, because your names are written in heaven.

—*Luke 10:18–20*

He that believeth and is baptized shall be saved; but he that believeth not shall be damned.

—*Mark 16:16*

Ye have not chosen me, but I have chosen you, and ordained you, that ye should go

and bring forth fruit, and that your fruit
should remain: that whatsoever ye shall ask
of the Father in my name, he may give it
you.

—John 15:16

① *You'll Have the Spirit!*

And I will pray the Father, and he shall
give you another Comforter, that he may
abide with you for ever;

Even the Spirit of truth; whom the world
cannot receive, because it seeth him not,
neither knoweth him: but ye know him; for
he dwelleth with you, and shall be in you.

I will not leave you comfortless: I will
come to you.

Yet a little while, and the world seeth me
no more; but ye see me: because I live, ye
shall live also.

At that day ye shall know that I am in my
Father, and ye in me, and I in you.

—John 14:16–20

These things have I spoken unto you,
being yet present with you.

But the Comforter, which is the Holy Ghost, whom the Father will send in my name, he shall teach you all things, and bring all things to your remembrance, whatsoever I have said unto you.

—*John 14:25–26*

But when the Comforter is come, whom I will send unto you from the Father, even the Spirit of truth, which proceedeth from the Father, he shall testify of me:

And ye also shall bear witness, because ye have been with me from the beginning.

—*John 15:26–27*

Nevertheless I tell you the truth; It is expedient for you that I go away: for if I go not away, the Comforter will not come unto you; but if I depart, I will send him unto you.

And when he is come, he will reprove the world of sin, and of righteousness, and of judgment:

Of sin, because they believe not on me;

Of righteousness, because I go to my Father, and ye see me no more;

Of judgment, because the prince of this world is judged.

I have yet many things to say unto you, but ye cannot bear them now.

Howbeit when he, the Spirit of truth, is come, he will guide you into all truth: for he shall not speak of himself; but whatsoever he shall hear, that shall he speak: and he will shew you things to come.

He shall glorify me: for he shall receive of mine, and shall shew it unto you.

All things that the Father hath are mine: therefore said I, that he shall take of mine, and shall shew it unto you.

—John 16:7–15

Behold, I send the promise of my Father upon you: but tarry ye in the city of Jerusalem, until ye be endued with power from on high.

—Luke 24:49

For John truly baptized with water; but ye shall be baptized with the Holy Ghost not many days hence.

When they therefore were come together, they asked of him, saying, Lord, wilt thou at this time restore again the kingdom to Israel?

And he said unto them, It is not for you to know the times or the seasons, which the Father hath put in his own power.

But ye shall receive power, after that the Holy Ghost is come upon you: and ye shall be witnesses unto me both in Jerusalem, and in all Judaea, and in Samaria, and unto the uttermost part of the earth.

—Acts 1:5–8

You'll Have Great Reward!

Blessed are ye, when men shall revile you, and persecute you, and shall say all manner of evil against you falsely, for my sake.

Rejoice, and be exceeding glad for great is your reward in heaven: for so persecuted they the prophets which were before you.

—Matthew 5:11–12

Blessed are ye, when men shall hate you, and when they shall separate you from their company, and shall reproach you, and cast out your name as evil, for the Son of man's sake.

Rejoice ye in that day, and leap for joy: for, behold, your reward is great in heaven: for in the like manner did their fathers unto the prophets.

—*Luke 6:22–23*

Take heed that ye do not your alms before men, to be seen of them: otherwise ye have no reward of your Father which is in heaven.

Therefore when thou doest thine alms, do not sound a trumpet before thee, as the hypocrites do in the synagogues and in the streets, that they may have glory of men. Verily I say unto you, They have their reward.

But when thou doest alms, let not thy left hand know what thy right hand doeth:

That thine alms may be in secret: and thy Father which seeth in secret himself shall reward thee openly.

—*Matthew 6:1–4*

And every one that hath forsaken houses, or brethren, or sisters, or father, or mother, or wife, or children, or lands, for my name's sake, shall receive an hundredfold, and shall inherit everlasting life.

—*Matthew 19:29*

Five

His Second Coming Is Getting Closer

*W*ill *Jesus return this year? Or the next? We don't know. The only thing for certain is this: His coming is closer to us than it was last year. Or than it was yesterday. It will be a surprise to us when He comes. But there are certainly things we can learn about all the events surrounding that cataclysmic event.*

Jesus Spoke of the End of the Age

Not knowing when the dawn will come I open every door.

—Emily Dickinson

And Jesus said unto them, See ye not all these things? verily I say unto you, There shall not be left here one stone upon another, that shall not be thrown down.

And as he sat upon the mount of Olives, the disciples came unto him privately, saying, Tell us, when shall these things be? and what shall be the sign of thy coming, and of the end of the world?

And Jesus answered and said unto them, Take heed that no man deceive you.

For many shall come in my name, saying, I am Christ; and shall deceive many.

And ye shall hear of wars and rumours of wars: see that ye be not troubled: for all these things must come to pass, but the end is not yet.

For nation shall rise against nation, and kingdom against kingdom: and there shall be famines, and pestilences, and earthquakes, in divers places.

All these are the beginning of sorrows.

Then shall they deliver you up to be afflicted, and shall kill you: and ye shall be hated of all nations for my name's sake.

And then shall many be offended, and shall betray one another, and shall hate one another.

And many false prophets shall rise, and shall deceive many.

And because iniquity shall abound, the love of many shall wax cold.

But he that shall endure unto the end, the same shall be saved.

And this gospel of the kingdom shall be preached in all the world for a witness unto all nations; and then shall the end come.

—*Matthew 24:2–14*

But when ye shall see the abomination of desolation, spoken of by Daniel the prophet, standing where it ought not, (let him that readeth understand,) then let them that be in Judaea flee to the mountains:

And let him that is on the housetop not go down into the house, neither enter therein, to take any thing out of his house:

And let him that is in the field not turn back again for to take up his garment.

But woe to them that are with child, and to them that give suck in those days!

And pray ye that your flight be not in the winter.

For in those days shall be affliction, such as was not from the beginning of the creation which God created unto this time, neither shall be.

And except that the Lord had shortened those days, no flesh should be saved: but for the elect's sake, whom he hath chosen, he hath shortened the days.

And then if any man shall say to you, Lo, here is Christ; or, lo, he is there; believe him not.

—*Mark 13:14–21*

For there shall arise false Christs, and false prophets, and shall show great signs and wonders; insomuch that, if it were possible, they shall deceive the very elect.

Behold, I have told you before.

Wherefore if they shall say unto you, Behold, he is in the desert; go not forth: behold, he is in the secret chambers; believe it not.

For as the lightning cometh out of the east, and shineth even unto the west; so shall also the coming of the Son of man be.

For wheresoever the carcase is, there will the eagles be gathered together.

—Matthew 24:24–28

◷ *So Look for His Return*

For I know that my redeemer liveth, and that he shall stand at the latter day upon the earth:

And though after my skin worms destroy this body, yet in my flesh shall I see God:

Whom I shall see for myself, and mine eyes shall behold, and not another; though my reins be consumed within me.

—Job 19:25–27

Our God shall come, and shall not keep silence: a fire shall devour before him, and it shall be very tempestuous round about him.

He shall call to the heavens from above, and to the earth, that he may judge his people.

Gather my saints together unto me; those that have made a covenant with me by sacrifice.

And the heavens shall declare his righteousness: for God is judge himself.

—Psalm 50:3–6

For, behold, the LORD will come with fire, and with his chariots like a whirlwind, to render his anger with fury, and his rebuke with flames of fire.

For by fire and by his sword will the LORD plead with all flesh: and the slain of the LORD shall be many.

—Isaiah 66:15–16

And his feet shall stand in that day upon the mount of Olives, which is before Jerusalem on the east, and the mount of Olives shall cleave in the midst thereof toward the east and toward the west, and there shall be a very great valley; and half of the mountain shall remove toward the north, and half of it toward the south.

And ye shall flee to the valley of the mountains; for the valley of the mountains shall reach unto Azal: yea, ye shall flee, like as ye fled from before the earthquake in the days of Uzziah king of Judah: and the LORD my God shall come, and all the saints with thee.

And it shall come to pass in that day, that the light shall not be clear, nor dark:

But it shall be one day which shall be known to the LORD, not day, nor night: but it shall come to pass, that at evening time it shall be light.

And it shall be in that day, that living waters shall go out from Jerusalem; half of them toward the former sea, and half of them toward the hinder sea: in summer and in winter shall it be.

—*Zechariah 14:4–8*

And then shall they see the Son of man coming in the clouds with great power and glory.

—*Mark 13:26*

In a moment, in the twinkling of an eye, at the last trump: for the trumpet shall sound, and the dead shall be raised incorruptible, and we shall be changed.

—*1 Corinthians 15:52*

And as it is appointed unto men once to die, but after this the judgment:

So Christ was once offered to bear the sins of many; and unto them that look for him shall he appear the second time without sin unto salvation.

—*Hebrews 9:27–28*

For the Lord himself shall descend from heaven with a shout, with the voice of the archangel, and with the trump of God: and the dead in Christ shall rise first.

—*1 Thessalonians 4:16*

Seeing it is a righteous thing with God to recompense tribulation to them that trouble you;

And to you who are troubled rest with us, when the Lord Jesus shall be revealed from heaven with his mighty angels,

In flaming fire taking vengeance on them that know not God, and that obey not the gospel of our Lord Jesus Christ:

Who shall be punished with everlasting destruction from the presence of the Lord, and from the glory of his power.

—*2 Thessalonians 1:6–9*

Behold, he cometh with clouds; and every eye shall see him, and they also which pierced him: and all kindreds of the earth shall wail because of him. Even so, Amen.

—*Revelation 1:7*

☉ *Recognize His Exaltation*

Let them praise the name of the LORD: for his name alone is excellent; his glory is above the earth and heaven.

—*Psalm 148:13*

For thou art the glory of their strength:
and in thy favour our horn shall be exalted.

—Psalm 89:17

Which he wrought in Christ, when he
raised him from the dead, and set him at his
own right hand in the heavenly places,

Far above all principality, and power, and
might, and dominion, and every name that
is named, not only in this world, but also in
that which is to come.

—Ephesians 1:20–21

For Christ is not entered into the holy
places made with hands, which are the
figures of the true; but into heaven itself,
now to appear in the presence of God for
us.

—Hebrews 9:24

Who is gone into heaven, and is on the
right hand of God; angels and authorities
and powers being made subject unto him.

—1 Peter 3:22

Saying with a loud voice, Worthy is the Lamb that was slain to receive power, and riches, and wisdom, and strength, and honour, and glory, and blessing.

And every creature which is in heaven, and on the earth, and under the earth, and such as are in the sea, and all that are in them, heard I saying, Blessing, and honour, and glory, and power, be unto him that sitteth upon the throne, and unto the Lamb for ever and ever.

—*Revelation 5:12–13*

And I fell at his feet to worship him. And he said unto me, See thou do it not: I am thy fellowservant, and of thy brethren that have the testimony of Jesus: worship God: for the testimony of Jesus is the spirit of prophecy.

And I saw heaven opened, and behold a white horse; and he that sat upon him was called Faithful and True, and in righteousness he doth judge and make war.

His eyes were as a flame of fire, and on his head were many crowns; and he had a

name written, that no man knew, but he
himself.

—Revelation 19:10–12

☝ *Honor His Kingship*

Tell ye, and bring them near; yea, let
them take counsel together: who hath
declared this from ancient time? who hath
told it from that time? have not I the LORD?
and there is no God else beside me; a just
God and a Saviour; there is none beside me.

Look unto me, and be ye saved, all the
ends of the earth: for I am God, and there is
none else.

I have sworn by myself, the word is gone
out of my mouth in righteousness, and shall
not return, That unto me every knee shall
bow, every tongue shall swear.

—Isaiah 45:21–23

Behold, the days come, saith the LORD, that
I will raise unto David a righteous Branch,
and a King shall reign and prosper, and shall
execute judgment and justice in the earth.

—Jeremiah 23:5

And the kingdom and dominion, and the greatness of the kingdom under the whole heaven, shall be given to the people of the saints of the most High, whose kingdom is an everlasting kingdom, and all dominions shall serve and obey him.

—Daniel 7:27

And set up over his head his accusation written, THIS IS JESUS THE KING OF THE JEWS.

—Matthew 27:37

And, behold, thou shalt conceive in thy womb, and bring forth a son, and shalt call his name JESUS.

He shall be great, and shall be called the Son of the Highest: and the Lord God shall give unto him the throne of his father David.

And he shall reign over the house of Jacob for ever; and of his kingdom there shall be no end.

—Luke 1:31–33

Then Pilate entered into the judgment hall again, and called Jesus, and said unto him, Art thou the King of the Jews?

Jesus answered him, Sayest thou this thing of thyself, or did others tell it thee of me?

Pilate answered, Am I a Jew? Thine own nation and the chief priests have delivered thee unto me: what hast thou done?

Jesus answered, My kingdom is not of this world: if my kingdom were of this world, then would my servants fight, that I should not be delivered to the Jews: but now is my kingdom not from hence.

Pilate therefore said unto him, Art thou a king then? Jesus answered, Thou sayest that I am a king. To this end was I born, and for this cause came I into the world, that I should bear witness unto the truth. Every one that is of the truth heareth my voice.

—John 18:33–37

For David is not ascended into the heavens: but he saith himself, The LORD said unto my Lord, Sit thou on my right hand,

Until I make thy foes thy footstool.

—Acts 2:34–35

For he must reign, till he hath put all enemies under his feet.

—1 Corinthians 15:25

That at the name of Jesus every knee should bow, of things in heaven, and things in earth, and things under the earth;
And that every tongue should confess that Jesus Christ is Lord, to the glory of God the Father.

—Philippians 2:10–11

Which in his times he shall shew, who is the blessed and only Potentate, the King of kings, and Lord of lords.

—1 Timothy 6:15

He Will Come Again with Power and Glory

For lo! the days are hastening on,
By prophet-bards foretold,
When with the ever-circling years,
Comes round the age of gold.

—Edmund Hamilton Sears[1]

God, who at sundry times and in divers manners spake in time past unto the fathers by the prophets,

Hath in these last days spoken unto us by his Son, whom he hath appointed heir of all things, by whom also he made the worlds;

Who being the brightness of his glory, and the express image of his person, and upholding all things by the word of his power, when he had by himself purged our sins, sat down on the right hand of the Majesty on high.

—Hebrews 1:1–3

Wherefore God also hath highly exalted him, and given him a name which is above every name.

—Philippians 2:9

And the Lord shall be king over all the earth: in that day shall there be one Lord, and his name one.

—Zechariah 14:9

And he shall judge among many people, and rebuke strong nations afar off; and they shall beat their swords into plowshares, and their spears into pruninghooks: nation shall not lift up a sword against nation, neither shall they learn war any more.

—*Micah 4:3*

For the earth shall be filled with the knowledge of the glory of the LORD, as the waters cover the sea.

—*Habakkuk 2:14*

But who may abide the day of his coming? and who shall stand when he appeareth? for he is like a refiner's fire, and like fullers' soap:

And he shall sit as a refiner and purifier of silver: and he shall purify the sons of Levi, and purge them as gold and silver, that they may offer unto the LORD an offering in righteousness.

—*Malachi 3:2*

And the kings of the earth, and the great men, and the rich men, and the chief captains, and the mighty men, and every bondman, and every free man, hid

themselves in the dens and in the rocks of
the mountains;

And said to the mountains and rocks, Fall
on us, and hide us from the face of him that
sitteth on the throne, and from the wrath of
the Lamb:

For the great day of his wrath is come;
and who shall be able to stand?

—Revelation 6:15–17

And I will shake all nations, and the
desire of all nations shall come: and I will
fill this house with glory, saith the Lord of
hosts.

The silver is mine, and the gold is mine,
saith the Lord of hosts.

The glory of this latter house shall be
greater than of the former, saith the Lord of
hosts: and in this place will I give peace,
saith the Lord of hosts.

—Haggai 2:7–9

And he shewed me a pure river of water
of life, clear as crystal, proceeding out of the
throne of God and of the Lamb.

In the midst of the street of it, and on either side of the river, was there the tree of life, which bare twelve manner of fruits, and yielded her fruit every month: and the leaves of the tree were for the healing of the nations.

And there shall be no more curse: but the throne of God and of the Lamb shall be in it; and his servants shall serve him:

And they shall see his face; and his name shall be in their foreheads.

And there shall be no night there; and they need no candle, neither light of the sun; for the Lord God giveth them light: and they shall reign for ever and ever.

—Revelation 22:1–5

Six

The Days Ahead May Not Be Easy

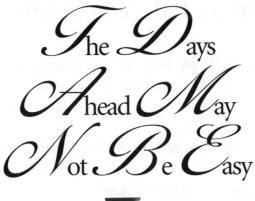

On our spiritual journey, the peace and maturity inside us can deepen as we walk in fellowship with the Lord, but the circumstances around us can deteriorate at the same pace. All the more reason to keep our faith fresh and strong!

Remember, Jesus Predicted Persecution

As in the physical world, so in the spiritual world, pain does not "last forever."

—Katherine Mansfield

Behold, I send you forth as sheep in the midst of wolves: be ye therefore wise as serpents, and harmless as doves.

But beware of men: for they will deliver you up to the councils, and they will scourge you in their synagogues;

And ye shall be brought before governors and kings for my sake, for a testimony against them and the Gentiles.

But when they deliver you up, take no thought how or what ye shall speak: for it shall be given you in that same hour what ye shall speak.

For it is not ye that speak, but the Spirit of your Father which speaketh in you.

And the brother shall deliver up the brother to death, and the father the child:

and the children shall rise up against their parents, and cause them to be put to death.

And ye shall be hated of all men for my name's sake: but he that endureth to the end shall be saved.

But when they persecute you in this city, flee ye into another: for verily I say unto you, Ye shall not have gone over the cities of Israel, till the Son of man be come.

—*Matthew 10:16–23*

The disciple is not above his master, nor the servant above his lord.

It is enough for the disciple that he be as his master, and the servant as his lord. If they have called the master of the house Beelzebub, how much more shall they call them of his household?

Fear them not therefore: for there is nothing covered, that shall not be revealed; and hid, that shall not be known.

—*Matthew 10:24–26*

If the world hate you, ye know that it hated me before it hated you.

If ye were of the world, the world would love his own: but because ye are not of the world, but I have chosen you out of the world, therefore the world hateth you.

Remember the word that I said unto you, The servant is not greater than his lord. If they have persecuted me, they will also persecute you; if they have kept my saying, they will keep yours also.

But all these things will they do unto you for my name's sake, because they know not him that sent me.

—*John 15:18–21*

These things have I spoken unto you, that ye should not be offended.

They shall put you out of the synagogues: yea, the time cometh, that whosoever killeth you will think that he doeth God service.

And these things will they do unto you, because they have not known the Father, nor me.

But these things have I told you, that when the time shall come, ye may remember that I told you of them. And these things I said not unto you at the beginning, because I was with you.

—John 16:1–4

Behold, the hour cometh, yea, is now come, that ye shall be scattered, every man to his own, and shall leave me alone: and yet I am not alone, because the Father is with me.

These things I have spoken unto you, that in me ye might have peace. In the world ye shall have tribulation: but be of good cheer; I have overcome the world.

—John 16:32–33

So Be Ready for Hard Times in the Latter Days

If you think of this world as a place intended simply for our happiness, you find it quite intolerable. Think of it as a place of training and correction and it's not so bad.

—C.S. Lewis

We are troubled on every side, yet not distressed; we are perplexed, but not in despair;

Persecuted, but not forsaken; cast down, but not destroyed.

—2 Corinthians 4:8–9

Wherein ye greatly rejoice, though now for a season, if need be, ye are in heaviness through manifold temptations:

That the trial of your faith, being much more precious than of gold that perisheth, though it be tried with fire, might be found unto praise and honour and glory at the appearing of Jesus Christ.

—1 Peter 1:6–7

No weapon that is formed against thee shall prosper; and every tongue that shall rise against thee in judgment thou shalt condemn. This is the heritage of the servants of the LORD, and their righteousness is of me, saith the LORD.

—Isaiah 54:17

For in the time of trouble he shall hide me in his pavilion: in the secret of his tabernacle shall he hide me; he shall set me up upon a rock.

—Psalm 27:5

Thou therefore endure hardness, as a good soldier of Jesus Christ.

No man that warreth entangleth himself with the affairs of this life; that he may please him who hath chosen him to be a soldier.

And if a man also strive for masteries, yet is he not crowned, except he strive lawfully.

—2 Timothy 2:3–5

For God hath not given us the spirit of fear; but of power, and of love, and of a sound mind.

Be not thou therefore ashamed of the testimony of our Lord, nor of me his prisoner: but be thou partaker of the afflictions of the gospel according to the power of God;

Who hath saved us, and called us with an holy calling, not according to our works, but according to his own purpose and grace, which was given us in Christ Jesus before the world began.

—2 Timothy 1:7–9

Before I was afflicted I went astray: but now have I kept thy word. . . . It is good for me that I have been afflicted; that I might learn thy statutes.

—Psalm 119:67, 71

Rejoicing in hope; patient in tribulation; continuing instant in prayer.

—Romans 12:12

⏱ *In Case You Feel Afraid*

The LORD is my light and my salvation; whom shall I fear? the LORD is the strength of my life; of whom shall I be afraid?

When the wicked, even mine enemies and my foes, came upon me to eat up my flesh, they stumbled and fell.

Though an host should encamp against me, my heart shall not fear: though war should rise against me, in this will I be confident.

—Psalm 27:1–3

Hearken unto me, ye that know righteousness, the people in whose heart is my law; fear ye not the reproach of men, neither be ye afraid of their revilings.

—Isaiah 51:7

There is no fear in love; but perfect love casteth out fear: because fear hath torment. He that feareth is not made perfect in love.

—1 John 4:18

In the mean time, when there were gathered together an innumerable multitude of people, insomuch that they trode one upon another, he began to say unto his disciples first of all, Beware ye of the leaven of the Pharisees, which is hypocrisy.

For there is nothing covered, that shall not be revealed; neither hid, that shall not be known.

Therefore whatsoever ye have spoken in darkness shall be heard in the light; and that which ye have spoken in the ear in closets shall be proclaimed upon the housetops.

And I say unto you my friends, Be not afraid of them that kill the body, and after that have no more that they can do.

But I will forewarn you whom ye shall fear: Fear him, which after he hath killed hath power to cast into hell; yea, I say unto you, Fear him.

Are not five sparrows sold for two farthings, and not one of them is forgotten before God?

But even the very hairs of your head are all numbered. Fear not therefore: ye are of more value than many sparrows. . . .

Fear not, little flock; for it is your Father's good pleasure to give you the kingdom.

—*Luke 12:1–7, 32*

⊕ *In Case You Feel Depressed*

Have mercy upon me, O LORD; for I am weak: O LORD, heal me; for my bones are vexed.

My soul is also sore vexed: but thou, O LORD, how long?

—*Psalm 6:2–3*

Come unto me, all ye that labour and are heavy laden, and I will give you rest.

Take my yoke upon you, and learn of me; for I am meek and lowly in heart: and ye shall find rest unto your souls.

For my yoke is easy, and my burden is light.

—*Matthew 11:29–31*

For ye have not received the spirit of bondage again to fear; but ye have received the Spirit of adoption, whereby we cry, Abba, Father.

The Spirit itself beareth witness with our spirit, that we are the children of God:

And if children, then heirs; heirs of God, and joint-heirs with Christ; if so be that we suffer with him, that we may be also glorified together.

For I reckon that the sufferings of this present time are not worthy to be compared with the glory which shall be revealed in us.

For the earnest expectation of the creature waiteth for the manifestation of the sons of God.

For the creature was made subject to vanity, not willingly, but by reason of him who hath subjected the same in hope,

Because the creature itself also shall be delivered from the bondage of corruption into the glorious liberty of the children of God.

For we know that the whole creation groaneth and travaileth in pain together until now.

And not only they, but ourselves also, which have the firstfruits of the Spirit, even we ourselves groan within ourselves, waiting for the adoption, to wit, the redemption of our body.

For we are saved by hope: but hope that is seen is not hope: for what a man seeth, why doth he yet hope for?

—*Romans 8:15–24*

And he said unto me, My grace is sufficient for thee: for my strength is made perfect in weakness. Most gladly therefore will I rather glory in my infirmities, that the power of Christ may rest upon me.

Therefore I take pleasure in infirmities, in reproaches, in necessities, in persecutions, in distresses for Christ's sake: for when I am weak, then am I strong.

—*2 Corinthians 12:9–10*

⏲ *In Case You Get Worried*

Be careful for nothing; but in every thing by prayer and supplication with thanksgiving let your requests be made known unto God.

And the peace of God, which passeth all understanding, shall keep your hearts and minds through Christ Jesus.

Finally, brethren, whatsoever things are true, whatsoever things are honest, whatsoever things are just, whatsoever things are pure, whatsoever things are lovely, whatsoever things are of good report; if there be any virtue, and if there be any praise, think on these things.

—Philippians 4:6–8

Peace I leave with you, my peace I give unto you: not as the world giveth, give I unto you. Let not your heart be troubled, neither let it be afraid.

—John 14:27

For you shall be as a tree planted by the waters, and that spreadeth out her roots by the river, and shall not see when heat cometh, but her leaf shall be green; and shall not be careful in the year of drought, neither shall cease from yielding fruit.

—Jeremiah 17:8

Thou wilt keep him in perfect peace, whose mind is stayed on thee: because he trusteth in thee.

Trust ye in the LORD for ever: for in the LORD JEHOVAH is everlasting strength:

For he bringeth down them that dwell on high; the lofty city, he layeth it low; he layeth it low, even to the ground; he bringeth it even to the dust.

The foot shall tread it down, even the feet of the poor, and the steps of the needy.

The way of the just is uprightness: thou, most upright, dost weigh the path of the just.

Yea, in the way of thy judgments, O LORD, have we waited for thee; the desire of our soul is to thy name, and to the remembrance of thee.

With my soul have I desired thee in the night; yea, with my spirit within me will I seek thee early: for when thy judgments are in the earth, the inhabitants of the world will learn righteousness.

—*Isaiah 26:3–9*

Now the Lord of peace himself give you peace always by all means. The Lord be with you all.

—*2 Thessalonians 3:16*

⏱ *In Case You Have Doubts*

Let us hold fast the profession of our faith without wavering; (for he is faithful that promised;) . . .

Cast not away therefore your confidence, which hath great recompence of reward.

For ye have need of patience, that, after ye have done the will of God, ye might receive the promise.

For yet a little while, and he that shall come will come, and will not tarry.

—*Hebrews 10:23, 35–37*

Verily I say unto you, That whosoever shall say unto this mountain, Be thou removed, and be thou cast into the sea; and shall not doubt in his heart, but shall believe that those things which he saith shall come to pass; he shall have whatsoever he saith.

—*Mark 11:23*

And this is the confidence that we have in him, that, if we ask any thing according to his will, he heareth us:

And if we know that he hear us, whatsoever we ask, we know that we have the petitions that we desired of him.

—1 John 5:14–15

And hereby we know that we are of the truth, and shall assure our hearts before him.

For if our heart condemn us, God is greater than our heart, and knoweth all things.

—1 John 3:19–20

Grace and peace be multiplied unto you through the knowledge of God, and of Jesus our Lord,

According as his divine power hath given unto us all things that pertain unto life and godliness, through the knowledge of him that hath called us to glory and virtue:

Whereby are given unto us exceeding great and precious promises: that by these ye might be partakers of the divine nature, having escaped the corruption that is in the world through lust.

And beside this, giving all diligence, add to your faith virtue; and to virtue knowledge;

And to knowledge temperance; and to temperance patience; and to patience godliness;

And to godliness brotherly kindness; and to brotherly kindness charity.

For if these things be in you, and abound, they make you that ye shall neither be barren nor unfruitful in the knowledge of our Lord Jesus Christ.

—2 Peter 1:2–8

◔ *In Case You Feel Tempted*

The Lord knoweth how to deliver the godly out of temptations, and to reserve the unjust unto the day of judgment to be punished.

—2 Peter 2:9

But the Lord is faithful, who shall stablish you, and keep you from evil.

—2 Thessalonians 3:3

Rejoice not against me, O mine enemy: when I fall, I shall arise; when I sit in darkness, the LORD shall be a light unto me.

—*Micah 7:8*

And the Lord shall deliver me from every evil work, and will preserve me unto his heavenly kingdom: to whom be glory for ever and ever. Amen.

—*2 Timothy 4:18*

The LORD shall preserve thee from all evil: he shall preserve thy soul.

The LORD shall preserve thy going out and thy coming in from this time forth, and even for evermore.

—*Psalm 121:7–8*

There hath no temptation taken you but such as is common to man: but God is faithful, who will not suffer you to be tempted above that ye are able; but will with the temptation also make a way to escape, that ye may be able to bear it.

—*1 Corinthians 10:13*

Likewise reckon ye also yourselves to be dead indeed unto sin, but alive unto God through Jesus Christ our Lord.

Let not sin therefore reign in your mortal body, that ye should obey it in the lusts thereof.

Neither yield ye your members as instruments of unrighteousness unto sin: but yield yourselves unto God, as those that are alive from the dead, and your members as instruments of righteousness unto God.

For sin shall not have dominion over you: for ye are not under the law, but under grace.

—Romans 6:11–14

Make not provision for the flesh, to fulfil the lusts thereof.

—Romans 13:14b

But Let Prayer Be Your Refuge

Thro' this world of toils and snares,
If I falter, Lord, who cares?

Who with me my burden shares?
None but thee, dear Lord, none but thee.

—*Christian hymn*

And, behold, a woman of Canaan came out of the same coasts, and cried unto him, saying, Have mercy on me, O Lord, thou Son of David; my daughter is grievously vexed with a devil.

But he answered her not a word. And his disciples came and besought him, saying, Send her away; for she crieth after us.

But he answered and said, I am not sent but unto the lost sheep of the house of Israel.

Then came she and worshipped him, saying, Lord, help me.

But he answered and said, It is not meet to take the children's bread, and to cast it to dogs.

And she said, Truth, Lord: yet the dogs eat of the crumbs which fall from their masters' table.

Then Jesus answered and said unto her, O woman, great is thy faith: be it unto thee

even as thou wilt. And her daughter was
made whole from that very hour.

—*Matthew 15:22–28*

Behold, the eye of the LORD is upon them
that fear him, upon them that hope in his
mercy;
To deliver their soul from death, and to
keep them alive in famine.

—*Psalm 33:18–19*

Seeing then that we have a great high
priest, that is passed into the heavens, Jesus
the Son of God, let us hold fast our
profession.
For we have not an high priest which
cannot be touched with the feeling of our
infirmities; but was in all points tempted
like as we are, yet without sin.
Let us therefore come boldly unto the
throne of grace, that we may obtain mercy,
and find grace to help in time of need.

—*Hebrews 4:14–16*

I will also save you from all your
uncleannesses: and I will call for the corn,

and will increase it, and lay no famine upon you.

And I will multiply the fruit of the tree, and the increase of the field, that ye shall receive no more reproach of famine among the heathen.

—*Ezekiel 36:29–30*

My help cometh from the LORD, which made heaven and earth.

He will not suffer thy foot to be moved: he that keepeth thee will not slumber.

—*Psalm 121:2–3*

And such trust have we through Christ to God-ward:

Not that we are sufficient of ourselves to think any thing as of ourselves; but our sufficiency is of God.

—*2 Corinthians 3:4–5*

Thou shalt make thy prayer unto him, and he shall hear thee, and thou shalt pay thy vows.

Thou shalt also decree a thing, and it shall be established unto thee: and the light shall shine upon thy ways.

When men are cast down, then thou shalt say, There is lifting up; and he shall save the humble person.

He shall deliver the island of the innocent: and it is delivered by the pureness of thine hands.

—Job 22:27–30

And Let Contentment Flow In!

All shall be well
and all shall be well
and all manner of thing shall be well.

—Julian of Norwich

Godliness with contentment is great gain. For we brought nothing into this world, and it is certain we can carry nothing out.

And having food and raiment let us be therewith content.

—*1 Timothy 6:6–8*

Let your conversation be without covetousness; and be content with such things as ye have: for he hath said, I will never leave thee, nor forsake thee.

—*Hebrews 13:5*

Two things have I required of thee; deny me them not before I die:

Remove far from me vanity and lies: give me neither poverty nor riches; feed me with food convenient for me:

Lest I be full, and deny thee, and say, Who is the LORD? or lest I be poor, and steal, and take the name of my God in vain.

—*Proverbs 30:7–9*

Behold that which I have seen: it is good and comely for one to eat and to drink, and to enjoy the good of all his labour that he taketh under the sun all the days of his life, which God giveth him: for it is his portion.

Every man also to whom God hath given riches and wealth, and hath given him power to eat thereof, and to take his portion, and to rejoice in his labour; this is the gift of God.

For he shall not much remember the days of his life; because God answereth him in the joy of his heart.

—*Ecclesiastes 5:18–20*

I know that there is no good in them, but for a man to rejoice, and to do good in his life.

And also that every man should eat and drink, and enjoy the good of all his labour, it is the gift of God.

—*Ecclesiastes 3:12–13*

Not that I speak in respect of want: for I have learned, in whatsoever state I am, therewith to be content.

I know both how to be abased, and I know how to abound: every where and in all things I am instructed both to be full and to be hungry, both to abound and to suffer need.

I can do all things through Christ which strengtheneth me.

—Philippians 4:11–13

For a day in thy courts is better than a thousand. I had rather be a doorkeeper in the house of my God, than to dwell in the tents of wickedness.

For the LORD God is a sun and shield: the LORD will give grace and glory: no good thing will he withhold from them that walk uprightly.

O LORD of hosts, blessed is the man that trusteth in thee.

—Psalm 84:10–12

Seven

God Has Plans for Your Future

We just aren't wise enough, or "in control" enough, to plan out a perfect existence for ourselves from birth to death. That's why "life engineering" isn't an option for the Christian. Instead, we place our future into the hands of God. He is all-wise and all-powerful—a great source of comfort! Yet the most consoling aspect of such an approach to life is this: being all-loving, our heavenly Father wants only the best for his children.

God Has Fantastic Plans for You

For each one of us, there is only one thing necessary: to fulfill our own destiny, according to God's will, to be what God wants us to be.

—*Thomas Merton*

As it is written, Eye hath not seen, nor ear heard, neither have entered into the heart of man, the things which God hath prepared for them that love him.

—*1 Corinthians 2:9*

For I know the thoughts that I think toward you, saith the Lord, thoughts of peace, and not of evil, to give you an expected end.

—*Jeremiah 29:11*

But God, who is rich in mercy, for his great love wherewith he loved us,

Even when we were dead in sins, hath quickened us together with Christ, (by grace ye are saved;)

And hath raised us up together, and made us sit together in heavenly places in Christ Jesus.

—Ephesians 2:4–6

For we know that if our earthly house of this tabernacle were dissolved, we have a building of God, an house not made with hands, eternal in the heavens.

For in this we groan, earnestly desiring to be clothed upon with our house which is from heaven:

If so be that being clothed we shall not be found naked.

For we that are in this tabernacle do groan, being burdened: not for that we would be unclothed, but clothed upon, that mortality might be swallowed up of life.

Now he that hath wrought us for the selfsame thing is God, who also hath given unto us the earnest of the Spirit.

Therefore we are always confident, knowing that, whilst we are at home in the body, we are absent from the Lord:

(For we walk by faith, not by sight:)

We are confident, I say, and willing rather to be absent from the body, and to be present with the Lord.

—*2 Corinthians 5:1–8*

For our conversation is in heaven; from whence also we look for the Saviour, the Lord Jesus Christ:

Who shall change our vile body, that it may be fashioned like unto his glorious body, according to the working whereby he is able even to subdue all things unto himself.

—*Philippians 3:20–21*

Knowing in yourselves that ye have in heaven a better and an enduring substance.

Cast not away therefore your confidence, which hath great recompence of reward.

For ye have need of patience, that, after ye have done the will of God, ye might receive the promise.

For yet a little while, and he that shall come will come, and will not tarry.

Now the just shall live by faith: but if any man draw back, my soul shall have no pleasure in him.

But we are not of them who draw back unto perdition; but of them that believe to the saving of the soul.

—*Hebrews 10:34b–39*

For we know in part, and we prophesy in part.

But when that which is perfect is come, then that which is in part shall be done away.

When I was a child, I spake as a child, I understood as a child, I thought as a child: but when I became a man, I put away childish things.

For now we see through a glass, darkly; but then face to face: now I know in part; but then shall I know even as also I am known.

—*1 Corinthians 13:9–12*

⏱ *Remember: You Are His Beloved Creation*

God created man in his own image, in the image of God created he him; male and female created he them.

And God blessed them, and God said unto them, Be fruitful, and multiply, and replenish the earth, and subdue it: and have dominion over the fish of the sea, and over the fowl of the air, and over every living thing that moveth upon the earth.

And God said, Behold, I have given you every herb bearing seed, which is upon the face of all the earth, and every tree, in the which is the fruit of a tree yielding seed; to you it shall be for meat.

And to every beast of the earth, and to every fowl of the air, and to every thing that creepeth upon the earth, wherein there is life, I have given every green herb for meat: and it was so.

And God saw every thing that he had made, and, behold, it was very good. And the evening and the morning were the sixth day.

—Genesis 1:27–31

I will praise thee; for I am fearfully and wonderfully made: marvellous are thy works; and that my soul knoweth right well.

My substance was not hid from thee, when I was made in secret, and curiously wrought in the lowest parts of the earth.

Thine eyes did see my substance, yet being unperfect; and in thy book all my members were written, which in continuance were fashioned, when as yet there was none of them.

—Psalm 139:14–16

For we are his workmanship, created in Christ Jesus unto good works, which God hath before ordained that we should walk in them.

—Ephesians 2:10

⊕ *As Your Father, God Blesses Your Future*

And God blessed them, saying, Be fruitful, and multiply, and fill the waters in the seas, and let fowl multiply in the earth.

—Genesis 1:22

And his father Isaac said unto him, Come near now, and kiss me, my son.

And he came near, and kissed him: and he smelled the smell of his raiment, and blessed him, and said, See, the smell of my son is as the smell of a field which the LORD hath blessed:

Therefore God give thee of the dew of heaven, and the fatness of the earth, and plenty of corn and wine:

Let people serve thee, and nations bow down to thee: be lord over thy brethren, and let thy mother's sons bow down to thee: cursed be every one that curseth thee, and blessed be he that blesseth thee.

—Genesis 27:26–29

And Israel beheld Joseph's sons, and said, Who are these?

And Joseph said unto his father, They are my sons, whom God hath given me in this place. And he said, Bring them, I pray thee, unto me, and I will bless them.

Now the eyes of Israel were dim for age, so that he could not see. And he brought them near unto him; and he kissed them, and embraced them.

And Israel said unto Joseph, I had not thought to see thy face: and, lo, God hath shewed me also thy seed.

And Joseph brought them out from between his knees, and he bowed himself with his face to the earth.

And Joseph took them both, Ephraim in his right hand toward Israel's left hand, and Manasseh in his left hand toward Israel's right hand, and brought them near unto him.

And Israel stretched out his right hand, and laid it upon Ephraim's head, who was the younger, and his left hand upon Manasseh's head, guiding his hands wittingly; for Manasseh was the firstborn.

And he blessed Joseph, and said, God, before whom my fathers Abraham and Isaac did walk, the God which fed me all my life long unto this day,

The Angel which redeemed me from all evil, bless the lads; and let my name be named on them, and the name of my fathers Abraham and Isaac; and let them grow into a multitude in the midst of the earth.

—Genesis 48:8–16

Speak unto Aaron and unto his sons, saying, On this wise ye shall bless the children of Israel, saying unto them,

The LORD bless thee, and keep thee:

The LORD make his face shine upon thee, and be gracious unto thee:

The LORD lift up his countenance upon thee, and give thee peace.

—Numbers 6:23–26

And Naomi said unto her two daughters in law, Go, return each to her mother's house: the LORD deal kindly with you, as ye have dealt with the dead, and with me.

The LORD grant you that ye may find rest, each of you in the house of her husband. Then she kissed them; and they lifted up their voice, and wept.

—Ruth 1:8–9

And he led them out as far as to Bethany, and he lifted up his hands, and blessed them.

And it came to pass, while he blessed them, he was parted from them, and carried up into heaven.

And they worshipped him, and returned to Jerusalem with great joy:

And were continually in the temple, praising and blessing God. Amen.

—Luke 24:50–53

⏱ *And He Gives You His Peace*

Dominion and fear are with him, he maketh peace in his high places.

—Job 25:2

What man is he that feareth the LORD? him shall he teach in the way that he shall choose.

His soul shall dwell at ease; and his seed shall inherit the earth.

—Psalm 25:12–13

The wolf also shall dwell with the lamb, and the leopard shall lie down with the kid; and the calf and the young lion and the fatling together; and a little child shall lead them.

And the cow and the bear shall feed; their young ones shall lie down together: and the lion shall eat straw like the ox.

And the sucking child shall play on the hole of the asp, and the weaned child shall put his hand on the cockatrice' den.

They shall not hurt nor destroy in all my holy mountain: for the earth shall be full of the knowledge of the LORD, as the waters cover the sea.

—*Isaiah 11:6–9*

And he will destroy in this mountain the face of the covering cast over all people, and the vail that is spread over all nations.

He will swallow up death in victory; and the Lord GOD will wipe away tears from off all faces; and the rebuke of his people shall he take away from off all the earth: for the LORD hath spoken it.

—*Isaiah 25:7–8*

I create the fruit of the lips; Peace, peace to him that is far off, and to him that is near, saith the LORD; and I will heal him.

—*Isaiah 57:19*

Now the God of hope fill you with all joy and peace in believing, that ye may abound in hope, through the power of the Holy Ghost.

—*Romans 15:13*

And the peace of God, which passeth all understanding, shall keep your hearts and minds through Christ Jesus.

—*Philippians 4:7*

So Let God Comfort You in All Circumstances

God, I choose the whole lot. No point in becoming a saint by halves. I'm not afraid of suffering for your sake; the only thing I'm afraid of is clinging to my own will. Take it. I

want the whole lot, everything whatsoever
that is your will for me.

—*Therese of Lisieux*

In the multitude of my thoughts within me thy comforts delight my soul.

—*Psalm 94:19*

For he maketh sore, and bindeth up: he woundeth, and his hands make whole.

—*Job 5:18*

The LORD doth build up Jerusalem: he gathereth together the outcasts of Israel.

He healeth the broken in heart, and bindeth up their wounds.

—*Psalm 147:2–3*

Therefore all they that devour thee shall be devoured; and all thine adversaries, every one of them, shall go into captivity; and they that spoil thee shall be a spoil, and all that prey upon thee will I give for a prey.

For I will restore health unto thee, and I will heal thee of thy wounds, saith the LORD;

because they called thee an Outcast, saying, This is Zion, whom no man seeketh after.

—*Jeremiah 30:16–17*

The LORD is my shepherd; I shall not want.

He maketh me to lie down in green pastures: he leadeth me beside the still waters.

He restoreth my soul: he leadeth me in the paths of righteousness for his name's sake.

Yea, though I walk through the valley of the shadow of death, I will fear no evil: for thou art with me; thy rod and thy staff they comfort me.

Thou preparest a table before me in the presence of mine enemies: thou anointest my head with oil; my cup runneth over.

Surely goodness and mercy shall follow me all the days of my life: and I will dwell in the house of the LORD for ever.

—*Psalm 23:1–6*

And Live in the Light of Heaven

As a countenance is made beautiful by the
soul's shining through it, so the world is
beautified by the shining through it of God.

—*Friedrich Jacobi*

But ye are come unto mount Sion, and
unto the city of the living God, the heavenly
Jerusalem, and to an innumerable company
of angels,

To the general assembly and church of
the firstborn, which are written in heaven,
and to God the Judge of all, and to the
spirits of just men made perfect,

And to Jesus the mediator of the new
covenant, and to the blood of sprinkling,
that speaketh better things than that of
Abel.

See that ye refuse not him that speaketh.
For if they escaped not who refused him
that spake on earth, much more shall not
we escape, if we turn away from him that
speaketh from heaven.

Whose voice then shook the earth: but now he hath promised, saying, Yet once more I shake not the earth only, but also heaven.

And this word, Yet once more, signifieth the removing of those things that are shaken, as of things that are made, that those things which cannot be shaken may remain.

Wherefore we receiving a kingdom which cannot be moved, let us have grace, whereby we may serve God acceptably with reverence and godly fear.

—Hebrews 12:22–28

There remaineth therefore a rest to the people of God.

—Hebrews 4:9

Thomas saith unto him, Lord, we know not whither thou goest; and how can we know the way?

Jesus saith unto him, I am the way, the truth, and the life: no man cometh unto the Father, but by me.

—John 14:5-6

After this I beheld, and, lo, a great multitude, which no man could number, of all nations, and kindreds, and people, and tongues, stood before the throne, and before the Lamb, clothed with white robes, and palms in their hands;

And cried with a loud voice, saying, Salvation to our God which sitteth upon the throne, and unto the Lamb.

And all the angels stood round about the throne, and about the elders and the four beasts, and fell before the throne on their faces, and worshipped God,

Saying, Amen: Blessing, and glory, and wisdom, and thanksgiving, and honour, and power, and might, be unto our God for ever and ever. Amen.

And one of the elders answered, saying unto me, What are these which are arrayed in white robes? and whence came they?

And I said unto him, Sir, thou knowest. And he said to me, These are they which came out of great tribulation, and have washed their robes, and made them white in the blood of the Lamb.

Therefore are they before the throne of God, and serve him day and night in his temple: and he that sitteth on the throne shall dwell among them.

They shall hunger no more, neither thirst any more; neither shall the sun light on them, nor any heat.

For the Lamb which is in the midst of the throne shall feed them, and shall lead them unto living fountains of waters: and God shall wipe away all tears from their eyes.

—Revelation 7:9–17

And I heard a voice from heaven saying unto me, Write, Blessed are the dead which die in the Lord from henceforth: Yea, saith the Spirit, that they may rest from their labours; and their works do follow them.

—Revelation 14:13

And I saw a new heaven and a new earth: for the first heaven and the first earth were passed away; and there was no more sea.

And I John saw the holy city, new Jerusalem, coming down from God out of heaven, prepared as a bride adorned for her husband.

And I heard a great voice out of heaven saying, Behold, the tabernacle of God is with men, and he will dwell with them, and they shall be his people, and God himself shall be with them, and be their God.

And God shall wipe away all tears from their eyes; and there shall be no more death, neither sorrow, nor crying, neither shall there be any more pain: for the former things are passed away.

And he that sat upon the throne said, Behold, I make all things new. And he said unto me, Write: for these words are true and faithful.

—Revelation 21:1–5

Eight

Make Sure Your Priorities Are in Order

Yes, you're busy. But keep making time for all the things that really matter—your family, your church, and the needs of your community. After all, the values you live by determine the kind of person you will become . . . this year, next year, and in all the years to come.

Live by Biblical Values

The actions of [people] are like the index of a book; they point out what is most remarkable about them.

—Heinrich Heine

Be not conformed to this world: but be ye transformed by the renewing of your mind, that ye may prove what is that good, and acceptable, and perfect, will of God.

—Romans 12:2

If the world hate you, ye know that it hated me before it hated you.

If ye were of the world, the world would love his own: but because ye are not of the world, but I have chosen you out of the world, therefore the world hateth you.

Remember the word that I said unto you, The servant is not greater than his lord. If they have persecuted me, they will also persecute you; if they have kept my saying, they will keep yours also.

But all these things will they do unto you for my name's sake, because they know not him that sent me.

—*John 15:18–21*

Who is he that condemneth? It is Christ that died, yea rather, that is risen again, who is even at the right hand of God, who also maketh intercession for us.

—*Romans 8:34*

⏱ *Continue Growing in Faith*

With God nothing shall be impossible.

—*Luke 1:37*

If ye have faith as a grain of mustard seed, ye shall say unto this mountain, Remove hence to yonder place; and it shall remove; and nothing shall be impossible unto you.

—*Matthew 17:20b*

Now faith is the substance of things hoped for, the evidence of things not seen.

For by it the elders obtained a good report. . . .

These all died in faith, not having received the promises, but having seen them afar off, and were persuaded of them, and embraced them, and confessed that they were strangers and pilgrims on the earth.

—Hebrews 11:1–2, 13

For whatsoever is born of God overcometh the world: and this is the victory that overcometh the world, even our faith. . . .

And this is the confidence that we have in him, that, if we ask any thing according to his will, he heareth us:

And if we know that he hear us, whatsoever we ask, we know that we have the petitions that we desired of him.

—1 John 5:4, 14–15

① *Treat Others with Hospitality*

And the LORD appeared unto him in the plains of Mamre: and he sat in the tent door in the heat of the day;

And he lift up his eyes and looked, and, lo, three men stood by him: and when he saw them, he ran to meet them from the tent door, and bowed himself toward the ground,

And said, My Lord, if now I have found favour in thy sight, pass not away, I pray thee, from thy servant:

Let a little water, I pray you, be fetched, and wash your feet, and rest yourselves under the tree:

And I will fetch a morsel of bread, and comfort ye your hearts; after that ye shall pass on: for therefore are ye come to your servant. And they said, So do, as thou hast said.

And Abraham hastened into the tent unto Sarah, and said, Make ready quickly three measures of fine meal, knead it, and make cakes upon the hearth.

And Abraham ran unto the herd, and fetcht a calf tender and good, and gave it unto a young man; and he hasted to dress it.

And he took butter, and milk, and the calf which he had dressed, and set it before them; and he stood by them under the tree, and they did eat.

—*Genesis 18:1–8*

He that receiveth a prophet in the name of a prophet shall receive a prophet's reward; and he that receiveth a righteous man in the name of a righteous man shall receive a righteous man's reward.

And whosoever shall give to drink unto one of these little ones a cup of cold water only in the name of a disciple, verily I say unto you, he shall in no wise lose his reward.

—*Matthew 10:41–42*

Then said he also to him that bade him, When thou makest a dinner or a supper, call not thy friends, nor thy brethren, neither thy kinsmen, nor thy rich neighbours; lest they also bid thee again, and a recompence be made thee.

But when thou makest a feast, call the poor, the maimed, the lame, the blind:

And thou shalt be blessed; for they cannot recompense thee: for thou shalt be recompensed at the resurrection of the just.

—*Luke 14:12–14*

And his master said unto him, We will not turn aside hither into the city of a stranger, that is not of the children of Israel; we will pass over to Gibeah.

And he said unto his servant, Come, and let us draw near to one of these places to lodge all night, in Gibeah, or in Ramah.

And they passed on and went their way; and the sun went down upon them when they were by Gibeah, which belongeth to Benjamin.

And they turned aside thither, to go in and to lodge in Gibeah: and when he went in, he sat him down in a street of the city: for there was no man that took them into his house to lodging.

And, behold, there came an old man from his work out of the field at even, which was also of mount Ephraim; and he sojourned in Gibeah: but the men of the place were Benjamites.

And when he had lifted up his eyes, he saw a wayfaring man in the street of the city: and the old man said, Whither goest thou? and whence comest thou?

And he said unto him, We are passing from Bethlehemjudah toward the side of mount Ephraim; from thence am I: and I went to Bethlehemjudah, but I am now going to the house of the LORD; and there is no man that receiveth me to house.

Yet there is both straw and provender for our asses; and there is bread and wine also for me, and for thy handmaid, and for the young man which is with thy servants: there is no want of any thing.

And the old man said, Peace be with thee; howsoever let all thy wants lie upon me; only lodge not in the street.

So he brought him into his house, and gave provender unto the asses: and they washed their feet, and did eat and drink.

—*Judges 19:12–21*

Then Peter went down to the men which were sent unto him from Cornelius; and said, Behold, I am he whom ye seek: what is the cause wherefore ye are come?

And they said, Cornelius the centurion, a just man, and one that feareth God, and of good report among all the nation of the Jews, was warned from God by an holy angel to send for thee into his house, and to hear words of thee.

Then called he them in, and lodged them. And on the morrow Peter went away with them, and certain brethren from Joppa accompanied him.

—*Acts 10:21–23*

And when they were escaped, then they knew that the island was called Melita.

And the barbarous people shewed us no little kindness: for they kindled a fire, and received us every one, because of the present rain, and because of the cold.

—*Acts 28:1–2*

Be not forgetful to entertain strangers: for thereby some have entertained angels unawares.

—*Hebrews 13:2*

⏱ *Keep Following God's Ways*

Take heed to thyself, and keep thy soul diligently, lest thou forget the things which thine eyes have seen, and lest they depart from thy heart all the days of thy life: but teach them thy sons, and thy sons' sons;

Specially the day that thou stoodest before the LORD thy God in Horeb, when the LORD said unto me, Gather me the people together, and I will make them hear my words, that they may learn to fear me all the days that they shall live upon the earth, and that they may teach their children.

—*Deuteronomy 4:9–10*

These words, which I command thee this day, shall be in thine heart:

And thou shalt teach them diligently unto thy children, and shalt talk of them when

165

thou sittest in thine house, and when thou walkest by the way, and when thou liest down, and when thou risest up.

And thou shalt bind them for a sign upon thine hand, and they shall be as frontlets between thine eyes.

And thou shalt write them upon the posts of thy house, and on thy gates.

—Deuteronomy 6:6–9

Hear, ye children, the instruction of a father, and attend to know understanding.

For I give you good doctrine, forsake ye not my law.

For I was my father's son, tender and only beloved in the sight of my mother.

He taught me also, and said unto me, Let thine heart retain my words: keep my commandments, and live.

Get wisdom, get understanding: forget it not; neither decline from the words of my mouth.

Forsake her not, and she shall preserve thee: love her, and she shall keep thee.

Wisdom is the principal thing; therefore get wisdom: and with all thy getting get understanding.

Exalt her, and she shall promote thee: she shall bring thee to honour, when thou dost embrace her.

She shall give to thine head an ornament of grace: a crown of glory shall she deliver to thee.

—*Proverbs 4:1–9*

⏱ *Practice Initiative and Accountability*

I went by the field of the slothful, and by the vineyard of the man void of understanding;

And, lo, it was all grown over with thorns, and nettles had covered the face thereof, and the stone wall thereof was broken down.

Then I saw, and considered it well: I looked upon it, and received instruction.

Yet a little sleep, a little slumber, a little folding of the hands to sleep:

So shall thy poverty come as one that travelleth; and thy want as an armed man.

—*Proverbs 24:30–34*

For even when we were with you, this we commanded you, that if any would not work, neither should he eat.

For we hear that there are some which walk among you disorderly, working not at all, but are busybodies.

Now them that are such we command and exhort by our Lord Jesus Christ, that with quietness they work, and eat their own bread.

—*2 Thessalonians 3:10–12*

And that ye study to be quiet, and to do your own business, and to work with your own hands, as we commanded you;

That ye may walk honestly toward them that are without, and that ye may have lack of nothing.

—*1 Thessalonians 4:11–12*

Know ye not that they which run in a race run all, but one receiveth the prize? So run, that ye may obtain.

And every man that striveth for the mastery is temperate in all things. Now they do it to obtain a corruptible crown; but we an incorruptible.

I therefore so run, not as uncertainly; so fight I, not as one that beateth the air:

But I keep under my body, and bring it into subjection: lest that by any means, when I have preached to others, I myself should be a castaway.

—*1 Corinthians 9:24–27*

Let every soul be subject unto the higher powers. For there is no power but of God: the powers that be are ordained of God.

Whosoever therefore resisteth the power, resisteth the ordinance of God: and they that resist shall receive to themselves damnation.

For rulers are not a terror to good works, but to the evil. Wilt thou then not be afraid of the power? do that which is good, and thou shalt have praise of the same:

For he is the minister of God to thee for good. But if thou do that which is evil, be afraid; for he beareth not the sword in vain: for he is the minister of God, a revenger to execute wrath upon him that doeth evil.

Wherefore ye must needs be subject, not only for wrath, but also for conscience sake.

—*Romans 13:1–5*

⊙ *Choose Good Friends*

Blessed is the man that walketh not in the counsel of the ungodly, nor standeth in the way of sinners, nor sitteth in the seat of the scornful.

But his delight is in the law of the LORD; and in his law doth he meditate day and night.

And he shall be like a tree planted by the rivers of water, that bringeth forth his fruit in his season; his leaf also shall not wither; and whatsoever he doeth shall prosper.

The ungodly are not so: but are like the chaff which the wind driveth away.

Therefore the ungodly shall not stand in the judgment, nor sinners in the congregation of the righteous.

For the LORD knoweth the way of the righteous: but the way of the ungodly shall perish.

—Psalm 1:1–6

The righteous is more excellent than his neighbour: but the way of the wicked seduceth them.

—Proverbs 12:26

A froward man soweth strife: and a whisperer separateth chief friends.

—Proverbs 16:28

Make no friendship with an angry man; and with a furious man thou shalt not go.

—Proverbs 22:24

Faithful are the wounds of a friend; but the kisses of an enemy are deceitful. . . .

Ointment and perfume rejoice the heart: so doth the sweetness of a man's friend by hearty counsel.

Thine own friend, and thy father's friend, forsake not; neither go into thy brother's house in the day of thy calamity: for better is a neighbour that is near than a brother far off.

—*Proverbs 27:6, 9–10*

Keep Persevering for the Lord

When nothing else seems to help, I go and look at a stonecutter hammering away at his rock, perhaps a hundred times without a crack showing in it. Yet at the hundred-and-first blow the rock will split in two, and I know that it was not only that blow which split it, but all that had gone before.

—*Jacob A. Riis*

Take heed, brethren, lest there be in any of you an evil heart of unbelief, in departing from the living God.

But exhort one another daily, while it is called To day; lest any of you be hardened through the deceitfulness of sin.

For we are made partakers of Christ, if we hold the beginning of our confidence stedfast unto the end;

—Hebrews 3:12–14

This know also, that in the last days perilous times shall come.

For men shall be lovers of their own selves, covetous, boasters, proud, blasphemers, disobedient to parents, unthankful, unholy,

Without natural affection, trucebreakers, false accusers, incontinent, fierce, despisers of those that are good,

Traitors, heady, highminded, lovers of pleasures more than lovers of God;

—2 Timothy 3:1–4

For many shall come in my name, saying, I am Christ; and shall deceive many.

And ye shall hear of wars and rumours of wars: see that ye be not troubled: for all these things must come to pass, but the end is not yet.

For nation shall rise against nation, and kingdom against kingdom: and there shall be famines, and pestilences, and earthquakes, in divers places.

All these are the beginning of sorrows.

Then shall they deliver you up to be afflicted, and shall kill you: and ye shall be hated of all nations for my name's sake.

And then shall many be offended, and shall betray one another, and shall hate one another.

And many false prophets shall rise, and shall deceive many.

And because iniquity shall abound, the love of many shall wax cold.

But he that shall endure unto the end, the same shall be saved.

—*Matthew 24:5–13*

For the which cause I also suffer these things: nevertheless I am not ashamed: for I know whom I have believed, and am persuaded that he is able to keep that which I have committed unto him against that day.

—*2 Timothy 1:12*

And whosoever doth not bear his cross, and come after me, cannot be my disciple.

For which of you, intending to build a tower, sitteth not down first, and counteth the cost, whether he have sufficient to finish it?

Lest haply, after he hath laid the foundation, and is not able to finish it, all that behold it begin to mock him,

Saying, This man began to build, and was not able to finish.

Or what king, going to make war against another king, sitteth not down first, and consulteth whether he be able with ten thousand to meet him that cometh against him with twenty thousand?

Or else, while the other is yet a great way off, he sendeth an ambassage, and desireth conditions of peace.

So likewise, whosoever he be of you that forsaketh not all that he hath, he cannot be my disciple.

Salt is good: but if the salt have lost his savour, wherewith shall it be seasoned?

It is neither fit for the land, nor yet for the dunghill; but men cast it out. He that hath ears to hear, let him hear.

—*Luke 14:27–35*

And he said unto them, Which of you shall have a friend, and shall go unto him at midnight, and say unto him, Friend, lend me three loaves;

For a friend of mine in his journey is come to me, and I have nothing to set before him?

And he from within shall answer and say, Trouble me not: the door is now shut, and my children are with me in bed; I cannot rise and give thee.

I say unto you, Though he will not rise and give him, because he is his friend, yet because of his importunity he will rise and give him as many as he needeth.

And I say unto you, Ask, and it shall be given you; seek, and ye shall find; knock, and it shall be opened unto you.

For every one that asketh receiveth; and he that seeketh findeth; and to him that knocketh it shall be opened.

—*Luke 11:5–10*

Not as though I had already attained, either were already perfect: but I follow after, if that I may apprehend that for which also I am apprehended of Christ Jesus.

Brethren, I count not myself to have apprehended: but this one thing I do, forgetting those things which are behind, and reaching forth unto those things which are before,

I press toward the mark for the prize of the high calling of God in Christ Jesus.

—*Philippians 3:12–14*

Be not deceived; God is not mocked: for whatsoever a man soweth, that shall he also reap.

For he that soweth to his flesh shall of the flesh reap corruption; but he that soweth to the Spirit shall of the Spirit reap life everlasting.

And let us not be weary in well doing: for in due season we shall reap, if we faint not.

—*Galatians 6:7–9*

Wherefore seeing we also are compassed about with so great a cloud of witnesses, let us lay aside every weight, and the sin which doth so easily beset us, and let us run with patience the race that is set before us,

Looking unto Jesus the author and finisher of our faith; who for the joy that was set before him endured the cross, despising the shame, and is set down at the right hand of the throne of God.

For consider him that endured such contradiction of sinners against himself, lest ye be wearied and faint in your minds.

—*Hebrews 12:1–3*

Nine

Be Wise with Money and Investing

Why do we place so much importance on what we have—and on what we don't have? Perhaps the solution to this problem is to recall that all things are on loan to us from the true Owner. Maybe that will help us enjoy the good things we have . . . while we learn to relax our grip on them a bit, too.

Don't Worry about Your Finances

What are [riches] to God's Word, to bodily gifts, such as beauty and health; or to the gifts of the mind, such as understanding, skill, wisdom? Yet we toil for them day and night, and take not rest. Therefore God commonly gives riches to foolish people to whom he gives nothing else.

—Martin Luther

Therefore I say unto you, Take no thought for your life, what ye shall eat, or what ye shall drink; nor yet for your body, what ye shall put on. Is not the life more than meat, and the body than raiment?

Behold the fowls of the air: for they sow not, neither do they reap, nor gather into barns; yet your heavenly Father feedeth them. Are ye not much better than they?

Which of you by taking thought can add one cubit unto his stature?

And why take ye thought for raiment? Consider the lilies of the field, how they grow; they toil not, neither do they spin:

And yet I say unto you, That even Solomon in all his glory was not arrayed like one of these.

Wherefore, if God so clothe the grass of the field, which to day is, and to morrow is cast into the oven, shall he not much more clothe you, O ye of little faith?

Therefore take no thought, saying, What shall we eat? or, What shall we drink? or, Wherewithal shall we be clothed?

(For after all these things do the Gentiles seek:) for your heavenly Father knoweth that ye have need of all these things.

But seek ye first the kingdom of God, and his righteousness; and all these things shall be added unto you.

Take therefore no thought for the morrow: for the morrow shall take thought for the things of itself. Sufficient unto the day is the evil thereof.

—*Matthew 6:25–34*

⏱ Practice Good Stewardship

The earth is the LORD's, and the fulness thereof; the world, and they that dwell therein.

For he hath founded it upon the seas, and established it upon the floods.

—Psalm 24:1–2

And as soon as the commandment came abroad, the children of Israel brought in abundance the firstfruits of corn, wine, and oil, and honey, and of all the increase of the field; and the tithe of all things brought they in abundantly.

And concerning the children of Israel and Judah, that dwelt in the cities of Judah, they also brought in the tithe of oxen and sheep, and the tithe of holy things which were consecrated unto the LORD their God, and laid them by heaps.

In the third month they began to lay the foundation of the heaps, and finished them in the seventh month.

And when Hezekiah and the princes came and saw the heaps, they blessed the LORD, and his people Israel.

—*2 Chronicles 31:5–8*

Upon the first day of the week let every one of you lay by him in store, as God hath prospered him, that there be no gatherings when I come.

—*1 Corinthians 16:2*

Give, and it shall be given unto you; good measure, pressed down, and shaken together, and running over, shall men give into your bosom. For with the same measure that ye mete withal it shall be measured to you again.

—*Luke 6:38*

Cast thy bread upon the waters: for thou shalt find it after many days.

—*Ecclesiastes 11:1*

And Jesus entered and passed through Jericho.

And, behold, there was a man named Zacchaeus, which was the chief among the publicans, and he was rich.

And he sought to see Jesus who he was; and could not for the press, because he was little of stature.

And he ran before, and climbed up into a sycomore tree to see him: for he was to pass that way.

And when Jesus came to the place, he looked up, and saw him, and said unto him, Zacchaeus, make haste, and come down; for to day I must abide at thy house.

And he made haste, and came down, and received him joyfully.

And when they saw it, they all murmured, saying, That he was gone to be guest with a man that is a sinner.

And Zacchaeus stood, and said unto the Lord; Behold, Lord, the half of my goods I give to the poor; and if I have taken any thing from any man by false accusation, I restore him fourfold.

And Jesus said unto him, This day is salvation come to this house, forsomuch as he also is a son of Abraham.

For the Son of man is come to seek and to save that which was lost.

—*Luke 19:1–10*

And when James, Cephas, and John, who seemed to be pillars, perceived the grace that was given unto me, they gave to me and Barnabas the right hands of fellowship; that we should go unto the heathen, and they unto the circumcision.

Only they would that we should remember the poor; the same which I also was forward to do.

—*Galatians 2:9–10*

For I mean not that other men be eased, and ye burdened:

But by an equality, that now at this time your abundance may be a supply for their want, that their abundance also may be a supply for your want: that there may be equality:

As it is written, He that had gathered much had nothing over; and he that had gathered little had no lack.

—*2 Corinthians 8:13–15*

But whoso hath this world's good, and seeth his brother have need, and shutteth up his bowels of compassion from him, how dwelleth the love of God in him?

—*1 John 3:17*

Charge them that are rich in this world, that they be not highminded, nor trust in uncertain riches, but in the living God, who giveth us richly all things to enjoy;

That they do good, that they be rich in good works, ready to distribute, willing to communicate;

Laying up in store for themselves a good foundation against the time to come, that they may lay hold on eternal life.

—*1 Timothy 6:17–19*

As every man hath received the gift, even so minister the same one to another, as good stewards of the manifold grace of God.

If any man speak, let him speak as the oracles of God; if any man minister, let him do it as of the ability which God giveth: that God in all things may be glorified through

Jesus Christ, to whom be praise and dominion for ever and ever. Amen.

—1 Peter 4:10–11

What? know ye not that your body is the temple of the Holy Ghost which is in you, which ye have of God, and ye are not your own?

For ye are bought with a price: therefore glorify God in your body, and in your spirit, which are God's.

—1 Corinthians 6:19–20

⏰ *Practice Frugality*

And he gathered up all the food of the seven years, which were in the land of Egypt, and laid up the food in the cities: the food of the field, which was round about every city, laid he up in the same.

And Joseph gathered corn as the sand of the sea, very much, until he left numbering; for it was without number.

And unto Joseph were born two sons before the years of famine came, which

Asenath the daughter of Poti-pherah priest of On bare unto him.

And Joseph called the name of the firstborn Manasseh: For God, said he, hath made me forget all my toil, and all my father's house.

And the name of the second called he Ephraim: For God hath caused me to be fruitful in the land of my affliction.

And the seven years of plenteousness, that was in the land of Egypt, were ended.

And the seven years of dearth began to come, according as Joseph had said: and the dearth was in all lands; but in all the land of Egypt there was bread.

—*Genesis 41:48–53*

And when the dew that lay was gone up, behold, upon the face of the wilderness there lay a small round thing, as small as the hoar frost on the ground.

And when the children of Israel saw it, they said one to another, It is manna: for they wist not what it was. And Moses said unto them, This is the bread which the LORD hath given you to eat.

This is the thing which the LORD hath commanded, Gather of it every man according to his eating, an omer for every man, according to the number of your persons; take ye every man for them which are in his tents.

And the children of Israel did so, and gathered, some more, some less.

And when they did mete it with an omer, he that gathered much had nothing over, and he that gathered little had no lack; they gathered every man according to his eating.

—*Exodus 16:14–18*

A good man leaveth an inheritance to his children's children: and the wealth of the sinner is laid up for the just.

—*Proverbs 13:22*

He that loveth pleasure shall be a poor man: he that loveth wine and oil shall not be rich.

—*Proverbs 21:17*

Be not among winebibbers; among riotous eaters of flesh:

For the drunkard and the glutton shall come to poverty: and drowsiness shall clothe a man with rags.

—*Proverbs 23:20–21*

⏺ *Let the Peace of God Reign in Your Heart*

These things I have spoken unto you, that in me ye might have peace. In the world ye shall have tribulation: but be of good cheer; I have overcome the world.

—*John 16:33*

For he shall be as a tree planted by the waters, and that spreadeth out her roots by the river, and shall not see when heat cometh, but her leaf shall be green; and shall not be careful in the year of drought, neither shall cease from yielding fruit.

—*Jeremiah 17:8*

Approach Your Work with Joy

How boring these meaningless details!
Is this really what work is meant to be?
Can You make it sing again?
Put the spark back in my zeal?
Because I know that work is a blessed
privilege;
I don't want to be ungrateful.
But how boring the piles of paperwork,
how deadening the countless reports,
how fatiguing the endless round of meetings.
Yes, I need to feel it again, Lord—the joy.

—Gary Wilde[1]

Commit thy works unto the LORD, and thy thoughts shall be established.

—Proverbs 16:3

He that tilleth his land shall be satisfied with bread: but he that followeth vain persons is void of understanding.

—Proverbs 12:11

The hand of the diligent shall bear rule:
but the slothful shall be under tribute.

—Proverbs 12:24

Be thou diligent to know the state of thy
flocks, and look well to thy herds.

For riches are not for ever: and doth the
crown endure to every generation?

The hay appeareth, and the tender grass
sheweth itself, and herbs of the mountains
are gathered.

The lambs are for thy clothing, and the
goats are the price of the field.

And thou shalt have goats' milk enough
for thy food, for the food of thy household,
and for the maintenance for thy maidens.

—Proverbs 27:23–27

The ants are a people not strong, yet they
prepare their meat in the summer;

The conies are but a feeble folk, yet make
they their houses in the rocks;

The locusts have no king, yet go they
forth all of them by bands;

The spider taketh hold with her hands,
and is in kings' palaces.

—*Proverbs 30:25–28*

I have coveted no man's silver, or gold, or
apparel.

Yea, ye yourselves know, that these hands
have ministered unto my necessities, and to
them that were with me.

—*Acts 20:33–34*

But none of these things move me,
neither count I my life dear unto myself, so
that I might finish my course with joy, and
the ministry, which I have received of the
Lord Jesus, to testify the gospel of the grace
of God.

—*Acts 20:24*

Notes

Chapter 1

1. William A. Ward, *Quote, Unquote* (Wheaton, IL: Scripture Press, 1977).

2. E. Paul Hovey, *The Treasury of Inspirational Anecdotes, Quotations, and Illustrations* (Grand Rapids: Revell, 1987).

Chapter 2

1. Lucius C. Porter, *The Treasury of Inspirational Anecdotes, Quotations, and Illustrations*

Chapter 3

1. Josh McDowell, *Evidence That Demands a Verdict* (San Bernardino, CA: Campus Crusade for Christ, 1972).

Chapter 4

1. Charles Simeon, *The Complete Book of Christian Prayer* (New York: Continuum, 1995).

2. John R.W. Stott, *The Complete Book of Christian Prayer*

3. Origen, *The Complete Book of Christian Prayer*

Chapter 5
1. Edmund Hamilton Sears, "The Angel's Song," quoted in *12,000 Religious Quotations* (Grand Rapids: Baker, 1992).

Chapter 9
1 Gary Wilde, *Simple Prayers and Blessings* (Lincolnwood, IL: Publications International, 1998).